The Cubicle Crusher

---

12 Proven Ways to Earn 6 Figures from Home, Quit Your 9 to 5, and Live Your Dreams!

Jenny Callaghan

Limit of Liability/Disclaimer of Warranty:

inspired publishing

ISBN: 978-1-78555-047-8

I dedicate this book to the people who become or have become cubicle crushers. Life's too short not to love what you do and live your dreams.

I hope that the ideas in this book assist you on your entrepreneurial journey.

Table of Contents

How to read this book

If you're reading this book, then you're **different**. You want a different life for yourself. The reality is that simply by purchasing this book, you are ahead of all those people who whine and complain about their life but don't do anything about it. But holding this book in your hands unfortunately won't make you a six-figure entrepreneur. You will actually need to read the book and take action.

This book shows you that there are many different ways to earn an income from home and crush the cubicle. My goal for you is simple—read the way that most resonates with you, interests you and **take action**.

A number of these ways can be combined to provide you with an online business that has multiple income streams. This is certainly something to aim for. However, as tempting as it is to rush in and try a number of different ways at once, don't. It's like ordering from the menu at your favourite restaurant—there's many things you enjoy, but you can't eat them all at once. So, **focus on one way** until you become a master at that.

I'd love to hear your stories and feedback on the book, so visit me at www.thecubiclecrusher.com

Now, let's crush the cubicle!!

Introduction

For many of us, the thought of a new working week and a looming Monday morning fills us with dread. Personally, I seem to go into an instant state of stress, my body tenses up, and that calm, peaceful feeling I left my Sunday morning yoga class with instantly dissolves. Before Monday has even started, I'm already counting down the days and thinking about the next weekend, and the new working week hasn't even begun. Sound familiar? So why do I feel like this? Why do many of us feel like this? The answer here isn't really revolutionary. It's simple. I don't enjoy being in a job.

Why? The moment the alarm goes off on Monday morning, I don't feel like I own my time. I run around like a mad woman to get myself ready in order to catch the train and be at work at a certain time. Once I get to work, from the moment I arrive until I leave, I'm caught up in a world that I haven't created. I didn't start the company and I didn't create the job. Ultimately, I am given a set of responsibilities that are what someone else wants and needs. I feel like I don't have the freedom to design my life. I'm executing someone else's dreams. Not my own. Does this seem familiar? So what is it that I want? I'm searching for freedom, the ability to design my life. To work the hours I want to work, to take holidays when I want to take them, and to make my own decisions.

When you stop and reflect, we are conditioned from a young age about our careers. Questions such as 'What do you want to do when you grow up?' are all too common. Like any 6- or 8-year-old can really answer that question! So as young children, we provide answers such as Doctor, Fireman, Teacher, Vet, and Policeman because we've watched TV or a movie, or know someone who is working in one of those careers. Think about it, when did you last hear a child say "I want to be an entrepreneur"? Possibly this is because it's a hard word for a young child to say, although it's likely that the child hasn't been conditioned to think of any other work life than the typical path most of us take.

This conditioning continues through life with us completing school and then possibly going on to do further education at institutions such as university. For some of us, we might have a part-time job on the side to supplement our studies and our lifestyle. When we finish our education, we then embark on the daunting task of finding a job. Most of us hope we can get something that is close to what we studied, although more often than not, we simply take what we can get.

Then, we spend up to a **third** of our lives at work. In any week, we spend about 40 hours a week at work. Not to mention the commuting time on top of that, which will easily add two plus hours. Now let's face it, with the ease of technology and the ability to be connected 24 hours a day, most of us are spending time outside the 'paid' week doing additional work such as responding to emails, preparing reports or presentations, or generally trying to stay on top of things.

We also try to fit in family time, social time, leisure time, and relaxation. At best, we only get little bits here and there, forcing us to cherish whatever time we get. But no matter what time we get, it's never enough. Someone always wants more of us. What about time for *you*? Where's that in all of this? That's not too much to ask, is it?

At least we have our annual leave to look forward to, right? Hmmm…sort of. Whilst we are encouraged to take our annual leave, the irony for most of us is that we work like crazy to finish our work so we can take our holiday. We chalk up extra hours in the weeks leading up to our vacation. We put "out of office" messages on our email and set off to enjoy some well-earned downtime.

If we're really disciplined, we won't check our email while on vacation, but chances are for most of us, we can't resist a quick look here and there. Then we come back from holidays to email inboxes with anything from several hundred to several thousand emails. Our relaxed holiday vibes vanish as we spend countless hours attempting to sort out our emails and trying to get back on top of our work. It's like a merry-go-round—once you get on, you never really seem to get off. The only relief you get is that every once in a while, the merry-go-round slows down a little to make you feel like you are almost in control.

It's funny because when I was in high school, I wanted nothing more than to be in the corporate world. I wanted the job where I wore power suits, high-heeled pumps, and earnt the income that went with it. I wanted the commute, to inhale the atmosphere as I worked in the "big smoke", and I saw it as a badge of honour to say proudly "I'm so busy at work". Truth be told, it was all I could think of.

For most of us, we've been programmed to think that we will climb the corporate ladder and hence be in our corporate jobs forever. Well, at least until retirement—whenever that might be. For most of us, it's the career path our parents had. We imagine working our way up that ladder to the "C-Suite" or to be a Vice President or CEO. We don't understand there is a different life out there and we don't actually have to work for someone else.

We can enter the entrepreneurial world and create a life on our terms. Quite often, it's not until something happens in our corporate job or we simply get fed up with working for someone else that we start to seek a different life. We know there has to be more to life than **being in a cubicle** Now over 20 years after high school, I'm desperately seeking another way out. I'm not afraid of working, nor of working hard—it's just that I want to do this on my terms rather than on someone else's.

The world of work is changing

We can't ignore the fact that the world of work is changing. Technology is more prevalent than ever before and it's also becoming smarter. An app such as Xero can do the work previously done by accountants, and check-in kiosks at airports have reduced the need for check-in staff. We need to face the facts, technology is redefining jobs and automation technology is completing tasks previously done by people. Remember the introduction of automatic teller machines (ATMs)? Or what about the self-checkout at supermarkets?

According to research by McKinsey, "As many as 45% of the activities that people are paid to do can be automated by adapting already demonstrated technologies." You might think that automation is affecting those in lower-skilled, lower-wage positions, however even higher-paid occupations such as senior executives, senior managers, and CEOs have large amounts of tasks that can now be automated.

According to the Oxford Martin Report, 47% of total U.S. occupations will be obsolete in the next decade or two. The report ranks 702 occupations in order of those most likely to be automated. The jobs "least likely to be automated" were choreographer and dancer. Lucky for you if that's your choice of career. Although for most of us, the odds aren't in our favour.

Organisations are also changing their structure, moving from a full-time workforce to a contingent or part-time based workforce employed on a short-term basis to complete given projects. In a report by the U.S. Government Accountability Office, 40.4% of the U.S. workforce are contingent workers. Figures in Australia highlight that 86% of jobs created in the last year were part-time.

In a recent report by PwC surveying 10,000 members of the general population in China, Germany, India, the UK, and the U.S., "2 out of 5 people around the world believe that traditional employment won't be around in the future. Instead, people will have their own 'brands' and sell their skills to those who need them". It's pretty clear that the idea of full-time employment on a comfortable income is coming to an end.

It doesn't end there! If you think that's grim, consider this:

- Taxes are continuing to rise across the world
- Salaries in real terms have stagnated since the 1970s
- Pension schemes are diminishing and relying on them means a meagre existence
- Our debt is increasing

It seems that the rich get richer and the poor get poorer. Where is the middle class? **We're getting crushed!** Now, more than ever, *we need to take control of our future*. So how do we do that? We need to become more educated and we need to become entrepreneurs. The world of entrepreneurship offers us an opportunity to become more self-reliant and resourceful. It enables us to write our own pay checks, not be told what we're worth. It affords us the freedom to create our own destiny rather than cross our fingers and hope for the best, or worse still have other people make decisions about our life. The best thing we can do for ourselves and our families is to realise that we can write our own pay check. We have all that we need to create a life on our own terms. We can't continue to place our future in the hands of others and see what happens.

Still not convinced? Maybe you think that getting another job that pays more or offers more flexibility or better retirement benefits may be the option for you? I'm afraid there's no good news for you either.

According to Glassdoor for Employers, on average 250 resumes are received for every corporate job opening. Of those 250, only 4 to 6 people will get an interview, and well, we know that only 1 person will actually get the job.

And it gets better (or worse). In an article published by Forbes, almost 80% of jobs are found via networking and therefore are actually never advertised. So in theory, you won't know about most of the jobs out there. Oh, and add to that—recruiters only spend about 6-7 seconds viewing your resume. I don't know about you, but I certainly think my career and skills warrant a little more than a measly 6-7 seconds glance. Kinda makes it hard to stand out, right? Clearly, landing another job is going to be a rather hard 'job' in itself. Added to all of this is the average time it takes to fill a job opening—52 days. It's clear that finding a job can be a very time-consuming and frustrating experience for you and those closest to you.

Let's think about this some more. Every country has an unemployment rate, but they also have a *true* unemployment rate. Chances are this is on the rise. And what about the size of the workforce? The likelihood is that this is growing and there aren't enough jobs to soak up the increasing size of the workforce. What about under-employment? That is, those people working part-time but looking for more hours. Most likely, this is also increasing.

This isn't about getting all doom and gloom with you. It's simply about highlighting a cold, harsh reality. Put down the rose-coloured glasses and wake-up. Open your eyes to what is happening.

So what do you do?

Get up and go to work tomorrow morning?

Or think like an *entrepreneur*?

As an entrepreneur, you can take matters into your own hands and create a life you truly deserve. The freedom to choose how and when you work. No more morning commute! No more morning rush hour in your household as you run around like an crazy person (maybe, that's just me) herding everyone to school or work. No more overtime or extra hours for very little in return. No more limited vacation time.

Imagine being able to choose your own hours!

Imagine being able to work when and where you want!

18

Imagine being able to take your children to school and pick them up!

Imagine freedom from the 9 to 5!

Imagine earning six figures from home!

What would that do for you and your family? What would life be like?

If you are reading this book, then you are searching for a better way to live. You are searching for a life free from the cubicle. You are tired of working for someone else's dreams and want to start working on yours.

There are hundreds of ways to earn an income from your computer now that will allow you to crush your cubicle-dwelling job! So in this book, you'll find the stories and strategies of some successful cubicle crushers! **So, let's get crushing!**

Mindset

"Whether you think you can or think you can't,
you're right." – Henry Ford

Before you start discovering the ways to become an entrepreneur, one of the most important parts of your entrepreneurial journey is having the right mindset. It's the number one thing that separates successful people from everyone else. There's going to be setbacks and failures that test your mindset. As long as you treat them as something you can learn and keep growing from, you'll be successful. So here's my top tried and tested tips on getting your mindset right:

1. Get rid of any doubt

"Doubt kills more dreams than failure ever will" – Suzy Kassem

It's natural when you are starting something new or different that doubt will creep in. As doubt often starts in the mind, when your inner doubts arise, try to disrupt the thought pattern. Simply saying an affirmation to yourself such as *"I believe in myself"*.

When you find you are doubting yourself, think of all the times you have achieved what you set out to achieve, something else wonderful happened, or you benefitted from the experience.

2. Don't let fear get in the way, kick it to the backseat

Fear can really paralyse you and stop you from taking action. What you focus on grows. If you focus on fear, it will only expand. When you feel fear, instead of focusing on it, count to three and face it head on. Just jump in and be brave as it's never as bad as you imagine. Start to take intentional action and run towards your fears instead of away from them. Don't let fear be the reason you don't achieve your dreams.

3. Remove the "what ifs"

"'What' and 'if' are two words as non-threatening as words come. But put them together side by side and they have the power to haunt you for the rest of your life: What if?" – Letters to Juliet

Spending time worrying about "what if" keeps the mind focused exactly where it doesn't need to be. Try to spend time focusing on what you **do want** to happen. Every time you go to say or think "what if?", say to yourself, "so what!", which pushes the nagging thought away.

4. Get out of your own way

Stop self-sabotaging your success. Take a moment and listen to the way you speak to yourself, and think about the habits and behaviours you have. For example, do you start a diet and say to yourself "no chocolate allowed" only to find yourself eating chocolate that afternoon? This is self-sabotage.

Often, our thoughts and behaviour are tied together. Many times, it is these habits and behaviours that are taking us away from attaining the things we deeply desire. In every moment, we are taking action that moves us toward or away from our deepest desires, such as creating the life we want. Spend some time understanding which thoughts and actions are in conflict with your deepest desires.

5.   **Work through your crappy limiting beliefs**

Maybe you don't feel you truly deserve the success you are seeking. Spend some time and do a deep dive to know where these beliefs came from and then be able to move past them.

6.   **Stop holding yourself back**

Don't put your health and happiness on the backburner any longer. It's all about what's going on between your ears. Believe you deserve to achieve your goal. Visualisation can be a very powerful tool to help move you towards your goals. Take some time to visualise what you want and feel into the emotion you will experience in attaining this.

7.   **Contain your freak-out moments**

Your entrepreneurial journey can be a total rollercoaster of amazingness one minute and the next minute someone criticises you, which plummets you down. Accepts that this is part of the journey and don't spend too much time on the down. Pick yourself up and keep going.

8.   **Eliminate your fear of taking action**

You have to take action on your dreams. Nothing kills a dream quicker than inaction. You can have all the knowledge and skills in the world, but if you don't take action, then how do you expect to achieve anything? Commit to spending a certain amount of time each day on actions to move you closer towards your dreams. This could be listening to an entrepreneurial podcast, reading a motivational book, writing a blog post, or developing an action plan.

9. **Develop a daily mindset practice**

All you need to do is find 10-15 minutes a day to dedicate to your mindset practice. It can be saying affirmations or meditating or a combination of both. Your mind is like a muscle and needs to be strengthened. A daily practice develops a strong mind, which helps to keep you moving forward. You have to constantly feed your mind and remind yourself that you are great.

10. **Focus on the positive and be grateful**

You have the power within you to control your thoughts. So start focusing on what you have and be grateful for that. Take a few minutes each day to write in a journal what you are grateful for. This helps you to focus on the positive and when this happens, your life starts to change. Positive vibes you put out into the world always come back.

Rome wasn't built in a day and the entrepreneurial journey is a marathon, not a sprint, so work at your own pace. Too many people give up right before they would have experienced success. The key is that ordinary people just like yourself have had success, so get really determined and focused. Don't give up. You can do it!

"Nobody is going to give you permission to shine, except yourself." – Amanda Clarkson

---

Starting Your Business

"If you can't figure out your purpose, figure out your
passion. For your passion will lead you right into your
purpose." – Bishop T. D. Jakes

Why do you want to start a business?

In the introduction, we looked at some of the reasons why and
how the world of work is changing, and how times are getting
tougher. This showed you why you need to change your future
and the importance of becoming an entrepreneur.

But aside from these hard facts about the changing nature of
work, it's also important to think about your personal "why".
So consider:

- Why do you want to become an entrepreneur?
- What is your reason for wanting to establish a
  business?
- Why is it so important to you?

Getting crystal clear on your purpose provides a bigger 'why'.
As you set about establishing your business, knowing your
'why' will help to keep you focused and clear on the bigger
picture. It also helps to keep you from getting bogged down in
the day to day.

Put simply, your 'why' is your vision.

The Cubicle Crusher's Hot Tip:

Once you know your 'why' type it up and print it out. Be sure to place it somewhere easy to see. Refer to it daily for inspiration and motivation.

Setting up a business

There's so many things to do when setting up a business, so it's important you do research into the specific requirements for your country. The key requirements include:

1. Considering your business structure and type
2. Opening a business bank account
3. Checking your tax obligations
4. Registering your business name
5. Checking your legal requirements

You need to decide what business to start

Once you have your 'why', then the first step is to decide what business to start. In essence, **your business needs to solve a problem or offer value to people**. It could be service-based or product-based or a mixture of both. For example, social media management is a service-based business offering different packages, such as posting and monitoring on one platform (e.g. Twitter) or several platforms (e.g. Twitter, Facebook, and Instagram).

When thinking about what business to start, it's important to think about who you are as a person. Some people have a great awareness of themselves and some people need a bit of help. A strong advocate for this is Marianne Cantwell of **Free Range Humans**, who started a little blog that turned into big business, including dozens of online courses and a bestselling book translated into six languages.

Marianne's story

Like most of us, Marianne had what seemed on the outside to be a good career in media and city consultancy, yet she found herself thinking, "Isn't there more to life than living for the weekends?" She moved around from job to job hoping to find "the one". After reading up on every life changing idea out there and undertaking a personality assessment, Marianne started experimenting and figured out that she could actually create a bespoke career where she does lots of stuff she loves rather than chasing one thing forever.

She started on a path to do that and ended up quitting her job with no backup plan. Knowing she had to make this work, she started a few ventures, made some mistakes, and learned lots along the way. But within three months of launching, she had been quoted as an expert in a book. Marianne discovered she loved to write, so she started a blog, and this turned into her business and passion—Free Range Humans.

A Free Range Human is a person who has created a Free Range work life that suits them, gets paid to do what makes them come alive, and has decided to live their life every day, not just on weekends.

Personality or entrepreneurial personality assessments

Along with gaining greater insight into yourself, personality assessments also help to provide you with validation of who you really are as an individual. This is valuable to understand how you interact with others, and most importantly, helps you identify what type of business you would be most suited to.

There are free assessments online such as Myers-Briggs or Keirsey, however some may charge a fee:

- https://www.16personalities.com/free-personality-test
- http://www.keirsey.com/sorter/register.aspx

How do I test what I want to do?

So, you have an idea of something you want to do and what your business will be. Now it's important to test out your idea in small form to make sure you're actually going to like doing it. It's very easy to get excited by an idea and a life that we love the sound of, but in reality we don't like actually doing it. So Marianne recommends completing a challenge where you try out two different things.

So, say you want to educate women to be more confident in workplace situations. This idea can take many forms such as you writing eBooks, running global conferences, launching a network of women that connect with each other, or offering coaching. The first question to ask yourself is, "which of those sounds the easiest to you, so easy it almost feels like cheating?"

Whichever form feels natural and effortless to you, then your project is to go and do exactly that.

1. Test your idea in a small form, for example, write a short eBook.
2. Take that idea and turn it into a paid project, for example, sell the eBook.

Your success approach – what's the thing that feels so easy?

Often, people try to do things because they see other people on the internet doing them, however they are not being true to themselves. Even though what they are doing is right, they are taking actions that aren't in flow with who they are as a person. You should be seeking to find a sense of ease with the actions you are taking. When you are forcing yourself to do something, it becomes a struggle and others can sense that.

The greatest tip when you are starting out, regardless of whether it's your first $1,000 or first $100,000, is when there's an approach that feels like it's almost cheating because it's too easy, do it. It is your success approach.

Where have you had unexpected success in your life?

The next big thing to do is to look back over your life and look at those moments where you've had unexpected success, even in a small form. It doesn't have to be wild global success (that's fine, though). It could be as simple as what in your work have you been able to do very effortlessly and wish you could've done more of? Include those effortless tasks that brought you unexpected success, as this will be important as you grow your business.

You don't need to have a huge email list to be successful

People often think that to be successful with an internet business, you need to have a huge email list. This isn't necessarily the case. Marianne was running a successful full-time business when she had an email list of about 400 people, all of whom she had met in person through running workshops in London. What's more important is that you have a product or service that people will buy it when they see it, and when it's right for them.

> **The Cubicle Crusher's Hot Tip:**
>
> *You don't need a huge email list to be successful. What you need is a great relationship with your subscribers!*

Develop a timeline – focus your mind

An important part of building a business is to set a timeline for yourself with each step along the way. By doing this, your mind focuses and you start to take the action to move you closer to your achievement. For example, "I am going to run an event on this date and I need 10 people". This is also applicable to things such as coaching. Regardless of whether you offer a service or have a product to sell, get clear on what you want to achieve and by when. For example, "I want to coach 10 people by the end of the month" or "I want to sell $2,000 worth of products by the end of the month.

How do you turn your idea into something that's really significant?

The first thing Marianne tells people to do when they're ready to grow something is *shift their mindset* to think about what it's going to take to magnify this. Through the exercises, you have discovered you have something that sells. Now it's just a case of multiplication. There are lots of different strategies you can use to do this, for example, you could create an eBook, an e-course, or a membership site. This means your content can be appreciated by many thousands of people over the years and what's more, you reap the financial benefits.

Marianne's final tip

The biggest tip is to look for reasons why things are possible and prove to yourself it's possible by actually doing a small version of it. This removes doubt and gives you confidence you are on the right path. Whatever idea you're thinking of, no matter how complicated, there's always an opportunity to do it in a small way.

Once you've seen people smiling or heard them say thank you, and pay you for that service or product, then you know it's possible. If it doesn't work when you do it, then get curious about why, ask yourself what went wrong, and try again in another form. You have all you need to be successful. Know that if you're able to pick up and read this book, then you are fully capable of taking the steps needed to establish your business.

Let's start reading

Unsure which chapter to read? The list below will help you work out which chapter to read.

> *If you like social media, go to chapters 1 and 2.*
>
> *If you like writing? If so, try chapters 3, 4, and 7.*
>
> *If you like helping people, go to chapters 5, 6, and 11.*
>
> *If you like blogging, go to chapter 7.*
>
> *If you like ecommerce, go to chapters 8 and 9.*
>
> *If you like podcasts, go to chapter 10.*
>
> *If you like online business strategies, go to chapter 11.*
>
> *If you like membership sites, go to chapter 12.*

Where to find out more

You can connect with Marianne here:

- Website: www.free-range-humans.com or www.mariannecantwell.com
- Facebook: www.facebook.com/freerangehumans
- Twitter: www.twitter.com/freerangehumans
- Instagram: www.instagram.com/freerangemarianne

Chapter 1

Social Media Management

"Nothing happens until you decide. Make a decision and watch your life move forward." – Oprah

This chapter is for those who enjoy posting on social media platforms such as Facebook, Twitter, or Instagram. Most importantly, it is for those who love being social and enjoy connecting with others.

*

One way to become a cubicle crusher is by being a social media manager. A social media manager is someone who manages social media accounts for businesses.

Social media management is one of the *fastest growing careers* of today. This is largely due to the way businesses market to consumers, which has completely changed. No longer do businesses rely on the Yellow Pages, in-store advertising, or direct mail marketing. To really be effective in advertising strategies, businesses need online marketing and therefore social media savvy people like you to help them manage their social media accounts and build their online presence.

Of the 3.17 billion internet users, they have an average of 5.54 social media accounts. Social media users have risen by 176 million in the last year. There are 2.789 billion active social media users and 2.549 billion active mobile social media users. A whopping 1 million new active mobile social users are added every day! Break that down and it's 12 each second. A massive 60 billion messages are handled by Facebook Messenger and WhatsApp every day!

It's clear that social media is here to stay. What's more, it's a really important medium for communication, not just with each other, but for businesses to talk to consumers. Luckily, some of you really enjoy social media and find it a lot of fun. Imagine replacing your nine to five with income earned through social media! Getting paid to post on social media!

There are plenty of examples of people who have successfully created a six-figure social media management business, such as Andrea Vahl, Phyllis Kane, Rachel Pedersen, and Stuart J Davidson.

According to www.socialmarketingwriting.com, businesses are investing in social media managers, paying between $500 and $2,500 to get an account on a platform set up. For a complete social media strategy, the figures increase significantly, between $10,000 to $30,000. For social media consulting, the hourly rates a manager can charge are from $50 to $500. It's easy to see how you can earn a significant income as a social media manager.

34

One person who is known internationally as the go-to person for social media marketing is Corinna Essa. Corinna is the CEO of a very successful social media management business **Social Media Worldwide.**

Corinna's Story

With a university degree in TV production, Corinna couldn't imagine working in any other industry. After she was made redundant at age 25 in the middle of the financial crisis, Corinna realised she needed to do something different. With no job prospects on the horizon and mounting bills, she reached out to her brother Mark Anastasi. Mark is an extremely successful internet marketer and he encouraged Corinna to attend a seminar he was running on social media. A reluctant Corinna attended and listened to many strategies from all the different speakers. The one that resonated with her was selling other people's products on Twitter for a commission. This is called affiliate marketing.

So what is affiliate marketing you might wonder? According to Problogger, affiliate marketing is *"a way of making money online whereby you as a publisher are rewarded for helping a business by promoting their product, service or site."* Simply put, you earn an amount for referring a visitor who takes some kind of action such as buying something (other people's products). You are rewarded commission, which is often a percentage of a sale or a fixed amount per conversion. Your conversions are tracked when you use a link embedded with a code specific to you, which enables the advertiser to track where conversions come from (usually by cookies).

Corinna was able to get started straight away creating free Twitter accounts. She built the accounts up to 10,000 followers in four months and started promoting products from ClickBank. ClickBank is "a top 100 online retailer with 200 million customers. ClickBank sells digital products worldwide created by entrepreneurs. ClickBank delivers digital lifestyle products to customers in 190 countries." (www.clickbank.com)

Within three weeks of promoting products, Corinna had replaced the income she lost from working in TV. She then went to build her email list and create her own product, an online course called "How to Make $700 a Week from Affiliate Marketing on Twitter". Her first product launch in late 2011 resulted in 16 sales and a total of $15,492 overnight. Due to the success of her online course, Corinna was invited to speak at the social media summit and offered the audience her online course. Interestingly, no one bought it. Completely confused, Corinna asked the audience why not. The audience said very simply that they wanted to leverage the power of social media, but didn't have the time or the resources.

Corinna then asked the audience how much they would pay for a 'done-for-you' Twitter service. They said $300, so Corinna went on to launch this service, which unsurprisingly, had a huge demand. What started out as a Twitter agency led to Corinna's current business—Social Media Worldwide, which turns over $4 million per year.

Why is social media management so great?

❖ **Low start-up costs** – it's free to establish yourself on most social media platforms such a Facebook and

Twitter. The only costs you will have when establishing your business is your website.

❖ **Quick** – Your business can be launched within a short space of time.

❖ **Location independent** – you can work anywhere and anytime.

❖ **Loads of free online resources** – there are so many articles, courses, and free resources you can access. New information is being published daily and it can all be accessed at the touch of a button.

❖ **Getting paid to post** – it's a fun way to make money!

Corinna's tips on how to actually get started

1. **Start small and master each platform**

   Pick one platform such as Instagram and commit to learning everything you can about it.

2. **Build your audience**

   Post regularly (daily is best) to build your audience. If someone likes or favourites your post, return the favour.

3. **Use hashtags**

   For platforms such as Facebook, Twitter, and Instagram, *hashtags are important* and have been shown to increase engagement. Hashtags are a bit like keyword research. Use hashtags relevant to your business.

4. Monitor your results

Most platforms will have a way to monitor your results to see which posts are getting the most engagement from your audience. As you identify what works, do more of the same.

5. Share your results with people

Try different posts and approaches to build your audience. Share your results with your audience via a blog where you post screenshots or hold a webinar to talk about your results. From there, people will ask you for coaching and training. They will naturally want you to help them get results.

> **The Cubicle Crusher's Hot Tip:**
>
> The most popular type of social media content for engagement is photos! Adding images to your posts increases engagement.

6. Once you have mastered a platform, monetise your offering

It's now time to offer your services. A good way to do this is via the 'side-hustle' where you start building your business whilst you are still working in your job. The goal is to start small and gradually increase your income until you are comfortable to leave your job.

Put together a 'done-for-you' service. This could include getting new followers or building a business's social media account to 100 likes.

To get an idea of what this could include, I recommend checking out:

https://www.socialmediaworldwide.com/#pricing

7. Where do you find clients?

- Promote your service via word of mouth in your network of friends and family.
- Post your service offering on your social media platform and ask your followers to share.
- Invest in some paid advertising such as Facebook ads. Check out www.neilpatel.com. Neil is a top influencer on the web and his blog is an amazing resource.
- Check out network or meetup groups for businesses or entrepreneurs in your local area.

Corinna's tips on how to achieve the heights of success with social media management

1. Establish a blog or website

It's essential to have a blog or website where people can find you and what you offer. A blog is also another way to show your knowledge and expertise.

2. Create your own products

A great way to add another income stream to your business is create your own products. For example, you could create an eBook or online course, or hold a workshop. This will help to further establish credibility and help to position you as an expert.

3. Connect with influencers

Find other social media influencers and follow them to help increase your exposure and build your credibility. Top social media mavens to follow rated by Mashable are:

- Michael Stelzner of Social Media Examiner
- Amy Verson, an internationally renowned social media strategist

4. Link your social media with other touch points

Make sure you have your website in your social media profile. Ensure your email signature has your social media links included. You could even get business cards printed with both your social media links and website address. These will help to maximise your exposure and allow people to easily find you.

The Cubicle Crusher's Hot Tip:

As social media is about connecting with people, make sure you have a high-quality image to represent your business and your logo. It's important to create a great first impression!

5. Give VIP treatment to your audience on social media

It's important to look after your followers. Offer incentives and exclusive gifts (such as free report or a chapter of your eBook) to ensure they remain loyal and become brand advocates.

Where to find out more

You can connect with Corinna here:

- Website: www.socialmediaworldwide.com
- Facebook: www.facebook.com/smwonline/
- Twitter: https://twitter.com/smwonline

Courses and websites:

- **"How to start a social media business"** course by James Burchill: This is a very economical course! - https://www.udemy.com/socialmediasecrets/

- **Social Media Manager School** run by Andrea Vahl and Phyllis Kane: This course is more expensive, however there are so many fantastic resources offered - http://socialmediamanagerschool.com/
- **The Online Marketing Institute** offers a social media marketing certification -
- https://www.onlinemarketinginstitute.org/certifications/social-media-marketing-certification/.
- **Social Media Examiner:** This is the world's largest social media marketing resource - http://www.socialmediaexaminer.com/
- **Social Media Today:** A fantastic online community and resource for those who need to have a thorough understanding of all things social media related - http://www.socialmediatoday.com/

Relevant Article:

- **"How to become a social media manager"** article by The Work At Home Wife – https://theworkathomewife.com/how-to-become-a-social-media-manager/

Chapter 2

Affiliate Marketing with Twitter

"The difference between ordinary and extraordinary is that little extra." – Jimmy Johnson

---

This chapter is for those who are interested in building an audience and connecting with others for the purpose of selling other people's products.

*

The internet is filled with many opportunities to make money and become a **cubicle crusher**. You learnt in the last chapter that having a strong social media presence is an essential part of building a business. In the case of the social media platform Twitter, it could actually be a business in itself. There are a number of ways you can make money from Twitter, through links, sponsorships, and other strategies.

Twitter offers great money-making capabilities and opportunities. This chapter will focus on affiliate links because Twitter is number 1 for posting affiliate links.

So, what is Twitter?

Twitter is essentially a microblogging platform. With over 317 million monthly active users, Twitter is a social media platform that you can't ignore. "Twitter is a service for friends, family and co-workers to communicate and stay connected through the exchange of quick, frequent messages. People post Tweets, which may contain photos, videos, links and up to 140 characters of text. These messages are posted to your profile, sent to your followers, and are searchable on Twitter search." (www.twitter.com)

A few facts about Twitter:

- A post is called a "Tweet"
- Common features include: Retweets, Direct Messaging, Follow People & Trending Topics, Links, Photos, and Videos
- Twitter uses its network to connect ideas and topics
- It focuses on quick "real-time" information allowing people to use hashtags (#) to easily connect ideas and topics

How does affiliate marketing work?

Affiliate marketing is a very popular way to make money, although from the outside, it can seem mysterious and confusing at first. Firstly, you need to sign up to an affiliate program and select a product to promote. You promote the product to your followers via an affiliate link, which is a unique ID that identifies you as the person that generated the sale. When someone buys a product from your link, the affiliate program will process the order, take the money off the customer, and split it. You receive a percentage of the money for generating the sales and the rest goes to the product merchant. The affiliate program will pay the money directly to you. Your affiliate link never changes, so the affiliate program will always know when to pay you.

The commission can vary from small amounts of $30 up to thousands of dollars per sale. The amount of money you make will depend on how many people buy products from your links. You get to choose the products so you will know exactly how much you'll make per sale.

One person who has had enormous success with affiliate marketing is Mili Ponce, an international digital marketing strategist. She is the founder of Europe's number one social media marketing blog www.socialsongbird.com, which draws an average of 10,000 visitors per day.

Mili's Story

Born and raised in Peru, Mili was no stranger to entrepreneurship as her father ran a successful business. After school, she moved to London to attend university, but had to withdraw from her studies when her father lost his business. As she needed to earn enough money to support her parents and herself, Mili got four jobs, working around the clock with hardly any sleep. After a host of health challenges, she realised she couldn't keep working like this.

A friend encouraged Mili to get a 'normal' 9 to 5 job like the rest of us. She landed a role at Belkin working as one of their supervisors. Earning a good salary managing a number of people with a prominent company, she had a lot to be happy about. However, she still wasn't feeling fulfilled and the salary wasn't enough to enable her to live the life she wanted.

With the arrival of her daughter, Mili realised she needed to change her situation. She attended a three-day event called "The Millionaire Mind Intensive", which changed her life forever, and said to herself she would do whatever she had to do to make it. She found a course on Twitter through Google, so she gave it a go. Through it, she managed to make $500 online by promoting affiliate products to her followers.

Several months passed and a friend invited Mili to an "Internet Millionaire Bootcamp". She went along although she didn't understand anything about the content, which included building email lists, online marketing, and lead generation. She got chatting to a young guy who asked her how she was finding the event. She said blatantly she was finding it boring, though she told him she had managed to made $500 online by promoting affiliate products. She embarrassingly discovered that he was Mark Anastasi, the organiser of the event. Later, Mark called her to the stage and asked her to tell the audience how she had made money online. What happened next surprised her. By telling her story, as an ordinary person who tried something and made some money, she connected with the audience. Many people try for a year and don't make any money at all.

The audience's reaction encouraged Mili, so she then focused all her efforts on Twitter. She researched everything she could about Twitter, including how to get traffic, and tried many different platforms. During all of this, she was still working in her day job. In her second month online, she managed to make $1,700, and in her third month, $2,500. Her success rocketed from there and by month five, she had made $10,000 by running Twitter marketing campaigns for authors, speakers, and a variety of small businesses.

Why is affiliate marketing via Twitter so great?

❖ No upfront costs

Social media is a way for you to try affiliate marketing without any upfront investment.

❖ The value of internet marketing

Learning how to market online or internet marketing is *one of the most valuable skills* you need to crush the cubicle. The ability to market yourself, your products, and your business via internet marketing successfully will take you from your nine to five to a successful business. Affiliate marketing is one such form of internet marketing.

❖ Fast responses

Most people access Twitter via their smartphones, which means fast responses and greater engagement. Also, the 140-character limit means the messages on Twitter are shorter and easy to digest. This also means Twitter is fast and very beneficial for real-time news.

> **The Cubicle Crusher's Hot Tip:**
>
> The internet is here to stay. It is an essential part of people's lives. Millions of people are connected to the internet every day. Learning how to market to those millions is essential for any business.

Mili's tips on how to actually get started with affiliate marketing on Twitter

1. Determine your niche

You need to decide what niche you will focus on. It's advisable to start with something you are interested in or are passionate about. For example, your niche could be getting fit at home, paleo diets, making money from home, or getting Twitter followers. Try to get as specific as you an.

2. Set up an affiliate account

There's a number of affiliate programs around so it's recommended that you do some research. Which you choose will depend on which niche you are focusing on and therefore which program has products suitable. It's also advisable to understand their commission payments before signing up. A couple of the most popular ones are:

- <u>ClickBank</u> – one of the oldest and most popular affiliate programs. They have a massive marketplace and also offer optional paid training in the form of ClickBank University.

- <u>CJ Affiliate</u> – (was called Commission Junction) another popular platform that is very well respected and the most established. They attract serious affiliate marketers and advertisers. They have a huge variety of products, both digital and physical, for almost every niche.

- <u>Amazon or eBay</u> are other vendors you could promote any affiliate product through.

Now choose your products related to your niche.

3. Set up Twitter accounts

Create one to five Twitter accounts all in the same niche. Create each account separately, with a different name, picture, and bio.

Go to www.twitter.com and find the signup box. Follow the steps to open your Twitter account. The Twitter Help function will also take you through the set up in several easy steps (https://support.twitter.com/articles/100990).

Always include a photo as this helps people relate to you.

Choose a short, easy to remember username such as @firstnamesurname instead of @245678.

4. Start Tweeting

Simply click on the Tweet button located at the top of your screen on the navigation bar. The "Compose new Tweet" box will appear. Enter in your text, click "Tweet" and you are on your way. As you only have 140 characters, it's about writing tweets that capture your audience's attention—a bit like a news headline.

Figure 4.1

Figure 4.2

For each Twitter account, write between 20 to 60 tweets and start posting them. This will help you to look established, rather than a newbie.

5. Get followers

Once your accounts are ready, the next part of the work starts. In this part, you will do the following:

- Follow several hundred people every day
- Schedule around 10 tweets every day on each account
- Retweet 10 tweets per day
- Favourite 50 tweets per day

This will help you to attract lots of followers and assist you to start making money. You will need to this every day for all of your accounts in order to earn real money with Twitter. It should take 10 to 20 minutes. It is advisable to do this via:

- Tweetdeck, which is free
- Hootsuite or Mass Planner, which involves a cost per month

Resist the temptation to buy followers as they probably won't be genuine. You will often see posts from other users on Twitter who offer to sell you followers. Additionally, other users may seek you out and message you with an offer to get you thousands of followers. Stay away from these as the followers can be what's called "zombie" accounts. These are inactive accounts often with jumbled up letters and numbers as usernames, that is, not real users at all. In addition, Twitter may suspend your account if it thinks you are aggressively trying to increase your followers.

Mili's tips on how to achieve the heights of success with Twitter affiliate marketing

1. It's about relationships

Whilst Twitter might seem from the outset to be words on social media, behind any Twitter account is a person. It's therefore important to give your Twitter account the human touch. Ensure you upload a photo of yourself and include some information about you. This will help your followers to connect with you.

You also need to develop trust with your followers and to do that, you need to help your followers with beneficial suggestions. Inject your personality into your tweets with some humour or interesting facts.

2. Genuine recommendations

Above all else, you need to be offering your followers valuable content Most importantly, don't promote something you don't believe in! The balance for your tweets should be 65% content and 35% promotion. This helps to engage your followers and stop them from being annoyed. Your followers want to see value in your tweets, so don't come across as too "salesy" or you won't build meaningful connections.

3. The power of hashtags

It won't be long before you see a tweet with a # prefix. This is called a hashtag. They are useful categorising tweets and trending topics. By using a hashtag, it is easier to find and share information, which helps in building a community. Ideally, your tweets should always include a hashtag as this will help you to reach more people regardless of the number of followers you have.

There is a helpful program called Ritetag that gives you instant feedback on your hashtag choices. For example, you can type "weight loss" into Ritetag and it will tell you valuable information such as how many people are watching that hashtag and what country they are from. It will also give you instant feedback on the strength of your hashtag.

4. Link to your blog and build your list

To ensure you have great success with affiliate marketing on Twitter, it's more effective to tweet a link to one of your blog posts that includes an affiliate link, rather than tweeting the affiliate link directly. With the 140-character limit on Twitter, it can be hard to really do your affiliate product justice. It's more effective to write up a review of the product on your blog, provide a review covering pros and cons, share why the product is relevant to your readers, tell them who would benefit most, and then tweet a link to the review. The best approach with your review is to be honest and real, and offer quality.

The added benefit of having a blog is you can also build an email list of visitors. The idea is to offer something free for your readers such as a report or eBook in exchange for their email address. This enables you to build your email list and contact your readers directly with updates or exclusive offers. There is a lot of power in having an email list to help grow and sustain your blog, supporting you for years to come.

5. Post often and schedule ahead

The reality when operating in the internet marketing space is that with so many people on Twitter, it can be easy for people to forget you. So, you need to be posting regularly. Schedule your tweets with something like TweetDeck, as it allows you to spend 15 minutes entering your tweets and they will be sent out at the scheduled time. Your tweets should include how to information, tips, or information on your niche, as well as a promotional tweet with your affiliate link.

> *The Cubicle Crusher's Hot Tip:*
>
> *TweetDeck is one of the most popular social media management tools on the web. It helps you manage and post to your social networking pages or profiles.*

Where to find out more

You can connect with Mili here:

- Website: www.miliponce.com
- Facebook: www.facebook.com/miliponceoliver
- Twitter: https://twitter.com/miliponceoliver
- LinkedIn: https://au.linkedin.com/in/miliponce
- YouTube: www.youtube.com/user/miliponce

Courses and Websites:

- **"Twitter Marketing"** course by Juri Fab: There is a small investment - https://www.udemy.com/twitter-marketing-strategy-how-to-promote-clickbank/

- **"Making Sense of Affiliate Marketing"** course by Michelle Schroeder-Gardner of the award-winning personal finance blog *Making Sense of Cents* - http://makingsenseofaffiliatemarketing.com/?affcode=57702_qe56ghlm

Chapter 3

Writing Books

"So many of our dreams at first seem impossible,
then seem improbable, and then when we
summon the will, they soon seem inevitable." –
Christopher Reeve

This chapter is for you if you would like to pursue the dream of making a living out of writing. It's ideal for you if you enjoy writing as a form of expression, have an idea you are passionate about, and want to share it with the world.

*

The amount of money made from a book can vary substantially as it's all about how many copies you sell. If your book sells 10,000 copies, then it's considered successful. Average royalties via a traditional publisher are 10%. Even if you sell 10,000 copies of a $10 book, you're only walking away with $10,000. If you go the self-publishing route, then you will make a larger profit, however there will be a higher investment for you upfront with costs such as editing, design, and printing. The reality is that making money from books is challenging. So why write a book? The main reason to write a book is actually for the *opportunities* it brings such as speaking, consulting, or training programs.

Michael Hyatt, the former chairman and CEO of Thomas Nelson Publishers, the seventh largest trade book publishing company in the U.S. and author of *Platform: Get noticed in a noisy world*, says that "being a published author has done more for my career – and my income – than I could ever have imagined. It has opened doors of opportunity I couldn't have dreamed were possible".

Writing a book isn't easy and takes hard work and perseverance. However, if you have an idea you are passionate about, want to share with the world, and know others will find value in your idea, then do it—the money will take care of itself. When you are finished and the book has been published, nothing can replace that feeling of accomplishment. Brian A. Klems sums up the moment when he finished his book, *OH BOY, YOU'RE HAVING A GIRL: A Dad's survival guide to raising daughters*, with this comment, "I felt like a complete and utter badass".

One person who has created a living around writing books is expert Natasa Denman. Having written five books and co-authored another two, she developed a system where aspiring authors can complete their book in as little as 48 hours. Her Ultimate 48-hour Author program has helped over 120 people so far publish their books.

Natasa's Story

Natasa worked in the optical industry for about 12 years until an unfortunate situation occurred where her husband lost their franchise of Specsavers. This really changed the trajectory of her life. She felt a lack of stability and wanted to regain control of her life. She decided to undertake some study to be a Life Coach and learnt how to grow a business from home. While she was sold on the fact that she could earn six figures over two months, the reality is it took her 2½ years. After about 13 months in business, she wrote a book about weight loss called *The 12 Steps to Successful Weight Loss*. Publishing this book really helped to build her trust and intimacy with her audience rapidly.

Natasa lives by the motto of *fast, fun, fame*. These are her three key values. She likes things to be fast, she gets frustrated if anything takes too long, and she wants fame. Like any of us, she wants to be successful. A few years later, she collaborated with someone to write a book and they each committed to write half of the book. She wrote a few cheat notes on the book, they came together over a weekend to collaborate, and recorded a lot of the content of the book. As it turned out, they managed to get the book done in three hours. The book was then out on the shelves within 72 days.

Natasa had a lightbulb moment and she really set about developing a plan to do a full book within seven hours, and combined with some marketing knowledge, she came up with her Ultimate 48-hour Author program, which has helped over 120 people so far publish their books with a 100% success rate. This system enables aspiring authors like you and me to complete their book in as little as 48 hours.

Why is writing a book so great?

❖ A book is your blueprint to promote who you are and what you are about.

❖ **You only need life experience.**

> You can draw on your own experiences, the people you have met, and any adversity you have overcome, which all give you a voice that is entirely unique. Discovering the hidden corners of your personal experience to share can provide a powerful story that others can benefit from.

❖ A book helps to set you up and really get your business off the ground.

❖ **A book positions you as an expert and the go-to person on that subject.**

> Your book will provide a powerful platform for you to build your expertise and establish yourself as a credible source. It's a great way to introduce yourself to future customers and showcase your business and brand "you".

Natasa's tips on how to actually get started

1. Define your topic

> Brainstorm a list of topics you feel passionate enough to write about. In order to select a topic, it's helpful to think about what will your book do for someone reading it?

What problem will your book solve? What are you communicating or teaching with this book?

2. Who is your target audience? Why will they read your book?

Who will read your book? What will draw them in to read your book? What do you want them to walk away with once they have read it? *Be really specific about who your audience are* and know why they should read your book, as this will help to ensure it resonates with them.

3. Unpack your chapters

Begin to outline and scope out the chapters of the book. Each chapter might be an individual lesson on its own. Firstly, come up with chapter headings, and make them catchy and interesting. Then for each chapter, think about the format system. This system has four components: why, what, how and what if.

- Start by coming up with a compelling "why" someone should read the chapter. It helps to think of the benefits of the chapter. Try to come up with at least five.

- Next, think about what the chapter is covering. Introduce and define any relevant terms.

- Thirdly, come up with the "how", which is really three different ways to teach the what.

- Lastly, the "what if" covers the objections and responses that might arise. Try to come up with at least three.

4. Research, quotes, or fun facts

It's a good idea to support or enhance your material with quotes or fun facts as this helps to demonstrate your points and bring the book to life.

5. Have a plan

This is an important part of your book. Commit to writing a certain number of words each day and schedule in time to achieve this. You might start with 200 words per day for a week and increase this to 500 words. Regular writing practice helps you to develop a habit, which in turn helps you to achieve your goal.

6. Speak your chapters

When we speak, we use conversational language, which is simpler and easier for the reader to understand. When we write, we quite often confuse the reader as we try to overcomplicate things using fancy, big words that are unnecessary. Your reader likes it simple and easy to understand.

It's not complicated to record your chapters. You can use to record them using Audacity (http://www.audacityteam.org/). Alternatively, you can use the recording function on your smartphone.

Speaking your chapters takes some practice, so it's recommended to trial this to ensure you are comfortable speaking.

> **The Cubicle Crusher's Hot Tip:**
>
> *Write first, edit later. This helps you to keep a better flow without interrupting yourself by critiquing your work.*

Natasa's tips on how to achieve the heights of success when writing books

1. Leverage the power of networking

Once your book is written, it's all about sales. One of the best places to start selling your is through your "warm network". Your warm network is essentially people you know. Expand this to include friends of friends or acquaintances. Spread the word about your book.

2. Marketing

Use a combination of offline and online marketing to let people know about your book. *Use the power of social media* such as Facebook ads to advertise and generate interest. Get out from behind your computer and meet people face to face via local area meet-ups, network groups, writing groups, book clubs, library readings, or other community groups. This is invaluable as it enables people to see the face behind the name, connect with you, and feel your energy.

For more tips, go to -
http://www.yourwriterplatform.com/promote-and-market-your-book/.

3.   The power of seminars

As Mike Cernovich says, "People don't buy books. They buy books from you." It's really important to *tell your story behind the book*. Seminars can be a fantastic way to get out and promote your book. Essentially, these are low cost events that give you an opportunity to be in front of people and connect with them. A seminar can be held at a local restaurant, club, community hall, hotel, or even church.

For a handy checklist and tips on organising a seminar, go to https://www.thebalance.com/seminar-planning-checklist-1223789.

4.   Webinars

Webinars are a low-cost, low-risk way to connect with your audience. They are seminars conducted over the internet. You can easily set up a webinar online using www.gotomeeting.com and there is a free 7-day trial to get you started. You can promote the webinar via social media to your warm network and ask friends to spread the word. Although you won't gain as much rapport as a face-to-face event, you may sell a service.

5. Create a sense of urgency

Use your network and get all the people you know to purchase your book on Amazon, on a certain day and between certain times. This will help to drive your book to #1. You need to create scarcity and competition, adding urgency for people to buy your book, which in turn helps create momentum.

6. Reviews

One of the most powerful ways to spread the word about your book is *word of mouth*, and there's nothing better than reviews. Reviews are important as readers often check them out before deciding to buy. Put up a post on social media asking for volunteers to read your book and agree to provide an honest review. Send the eBook to them for free in exchange for their review. Reviews trigger the Amazon algorithms, which means they help to boost your book.

> *The Cubicle Crusher's Hot Tip:*
>
> *Books don't sell themselves. An important part of the marketing plan is getting reviews. A positive review says, "YES, this book is worth reading."*

Where to find out more

You can connect with Natasa here:

- Website: www.ultimate48hourauthor.com.au or www.natasadenman.org
- Facebook: www.facebook.com/natasadenman

Chapter 4

EBooks

"Entrepreneurs are willing to work 80 hours a week to avoid working 40 hours a week." – Lori Greiner

---

This chapter is for people who love to write and want to have a digital product to offer their audience. eBooks are not difficult to create and sell, even if you haven't written one before.

*

With technology here to stay and influencing every part of our lives, it has also changed the habits of book readers. Nowadays, instead of buying a hardcover or paperback book, you can purchase an electronic or digital book called an eBook, delivered instantly to your computer or handheld device. eBooks are an emerging market and are a great way to sell information.

Whilst paper books still outsell eBooks, the eBook market offers a viable way to make money. In the top five English language markets, eBook sales are as follows:

- In the USA, eBook sales represent 42% of all book sales
- In the UK, eBook sales represent 34% of all book sales
- In Canada, eBook sales represent 34% of all book sales
- In Australia, eBook sales represent 28% of all book sales

Can you be successful with eBooks?

The internet is filled with examples of many people who have managed to make their full time living from writing and publishing eBooks. One such person is Amanda Hocking, who wrote in her spare time while working full time as a disability carer. After receiving rejection letter after rejection letter from publishers and literary agents, she decided to self-publish her eBooks. In April 2010, Amanda made her first book available to Kindle readers on Amazon's website and also on Smashwords. By August that year, she had quit her day job. Amanda managed to sell 1.5 million books and made $2.5 million in a 20-month period. You can read more about her story here www.worldofamandahocking.com

Other success stories include:

- Louise Ross - https://www.ljrossauthor.com/
- Rachel Abbot - http://www.rachel-abbott.com/
- John Locke - https://johnlockeauthor.wordpress.com/
- Tracey Bloom - https://tracybloom.com/
- Paul Pilkington - https://www.paulpilkington.com/

One person who became a cubicle crusher and quit her day job due to consistent passive income earnt from eBooks is expert Sylvie McCracken.

Sylvie's Story

Sylvie knew she was destined to be an entrepreneur and no job would ever cut it. She had a full-time job as a personal celebrity assistant as well as being a wife and mother to three children. After a radical health change by simply altering her diet resulted in her losing 65 pounds and discovering a new-found passion for health and fitness, she realised she wanted to share this passion. She also had a deep yearning for some freedom in her life. She set two goals for her passion: 1) it would revolutionise her life and 2) she wanted it to be a business that made more than some coffee money. She set her target earnings at $60,000USD, which at the time felt impossible and out of reach.

With her goals in mind, Sylvie started a health blog and business called "Hollywood Homestead". With no prior knowledge of blogging or online business, she set about learning everything from WordPress to widgets. She worked evening and weekends on her blog. She only had 10 hours per week to spend on her blog, so she needed to use her time wisely and do things quickly. She started to outsource tasks for the small fee of $10 per hour, first delegating the simple tasks such as putting up a blog post. She also invested in herself through courses and mentors. Although hesitant at first to spend any money on a course, she knew it would save her months and months of learning.

When her blog was up and running, Sylvie started to look at what other bloggers were doing. She noticed some of them had eBooks, although they had huge amounts of traffic. Though she didn't have the same volume of traffic, she still set about creating an eBook. Six months after she started her blog, she launched her first eBook. Six months after that, she was making enough money from eBooks to be able to quit her job.

Why are eBooks so great?

❖ **Passive income**

The power of eBooks is that once they are created, *you continue to earn money over and over again.* Imagine waking up every morning with money in your bank account? This is the power of eBooks and you should be leveraging them to create an income and your ultimate lifestyle.

❖ **Great for your brand**

eBooks helps to increase your visibility and boost your authority in your chosen topic or niche.

❖ **Easier than physical products**

When you sell physical products such as clothes or books, you have to worry about things like warehousing, inventory, and shipping. There is none of that with eBooks—being digital, they are quickly and easily downloaded and into your customer's hands.

❖ **You can help more people**

Through an eBook, you get to share your knowledge and information, which will be able to help thousands of people.

❖ **Allow you to go into more depth**

Some topics can't be covered in a blog post or several bullet points. For those topics, an eBook is the perfect solution, allowing you to delve deeper into a topic and deliver valuable information in a neat and tidy package.

Sylvie's tips on how to actually get started

1. Select a topic

Choose what you will write about. Do some market research to check there is demand for it. Find out what problems people have.

2. Create an outline

Don't go straight into writing. Start mind mapping the information and creating an outline for the book. This will help you organise the information into a clear and concise structure and makes the task of writing seem less overwhelming.

3. Start writing

Commit to writing regularly, for example, you might want to write 1,000 words a day. It might sound like a lot, but once you get started, you'd be surprised how quickly you'll reach that target.

4. Edit, re-edit, and proofread

There will most likely be a few spelling and grammar mistakes. Be sure to read your eBook several times, on a different day to ensure you have a fresh perspective. You could get someone else to read it or consider getting a professional editor and proofreader to check the book. Whilst the latter may cost you, it's important to ensure you have a professional product.

5. Create a cover

It's important to have a striking cover that clearly identifies what your eBook is about. This will help it to stand out, particularly because books are displayed online with a thumbnail image of the cover design. Unless you are good at graphic design, it's worth finding a professional to design one for you. Check out Fiverr, Upwork, or 99designs.

6. Sell it

There are two ways to sell your eBook: by yourself or via distributors such as Amazon. Amazon is popular due to its large audience, although they will take a percentage of the sales. If you sell your eBook through your blog or website, you will keep 100% of the profits, however you will need to install a payment processor like eJunkie.

The Cubicle Crusher's Hot Tip:

Anywhere from 14,000 to 20,000 words is a good length for a non-fiction eBook. The most important thing is that your eBook delivers on its title.

Sylvie's tips on how to achieve the heights of success with eBooks

1. Seek feedback

Get feedback on your eBook from those you trust to be able to offer an objective point of view. Your best friend is probably going to give you positive feedback, which while great, isn't going to help you. Take on all feedback as even the smallest tweaks such as reordering your chapters may mean the difference between an eBook that sells okay versus one that sells extremely well.

2. Don't get married to your title

You have a great idea for the title of your eBook, however quite often it will evolve along the way. You could be 80 or 90% done before you actually decide on the title you will run with in the end.

3. Start marketing before you finish

Place the image of your eBook cover on your website as well as on your social media platforms. This helps to build anticipation and generate interest. Write a blog post or create a short video about your book with an email signup form. Once the book is ready, then you'll have a group of customers ready to buy.

4. Pick a price point

eBooks are a retail product and like any product in a retail store, prices vary. If you distribute your eBook via Amazon, then they have a pricing guide you'll need to follow. If you distribute via your website, then you have more freedom to price accordingly. There's no magic formula for pricing your eBook, although it's important to price it according to its worth. Some are priced at $2.99 USD whilst others are priced at $27 USD. Do some research to determine what price point will be best.

The Cubicle Crusher's Hot Tip:

You have to build excitement around your eBook. Use your social media to create a contest or giveaway a chapter. You could also post interesting content related to your eBook's topic.

Where to find out more

You can connect with Sylvie here:

- Website: www.sylviemccracken.com
- Facebook: www.facebook.com/sylviemccracken
- Twitter: www.twitter.com/sylviemccracken
- Instagram: www.instagram.com/sylvie.mccracken/

Chapter 5

Online Courses

"A dream doesn't become reality through magic, it takes sweat, determination and hard work." – Colin Powell

---

This chapter is for people with a love of teaching or instructing something. If you can take a topic and break it down into easy steps, then developing an online course to earn income is for you.

*

The world of online learning has made self-education so accessible. Thousands of courses are at your fingertips and what's more, you can take these courses at a time that works for you. All you need is a computer, a notepad, an internet connection, and an interest in your chosen topic. Who wouldn't want to learn from the comfort of their home, without any of the complexities of commuting to physical classes?

Aside from accessibility, online learning has really changed the way we learn and how we learn. Online courses fill the knowledge gaps, plus there's a course to suit every budget and every topic or interest. Not to mention, self-development and lifelong learning are growing trends.

From a business point of view, online courses are a great way to leverage your time and effort. You create them once and earn income over and over again. Course content can be offered via video, audio, or text—or a combination of all of them.

With online course sites such as Udemy, Teachable, and Thinkific, anyone can get started creating, marketing, and selling their online course. To help you understand what income you could achieve, here's a few success stories:

- Rob Percival posted his first online web development course in June 2014 for $199 USD. Within a few months, he was earning US$50,000 per month. He now has four courses on Udemy, which have taught 125,000 people and made him $1 million USD.

- Nick Walter made $66,533 USD in 30 days with his online courses, all this without having a full-time job.

One of the expert's in online course creation is Sarah Cordiner of **Main Training**. Sarah has been named one of the 50 must-follow women entrepreneurs in 2017 in Huffington Post and has created numerous online courses.

Sarah's Story

Sarah's story is a bit of a rollercoaster, but also of **self-made success**. She had just started her career as a trainer in the welfare-to-work industry and was still studying for her degree in curriculum design when she was told she was being made redundant. She realised people still needed her skills and set about starting her first business aged 19, with no money and very limited experience. Despite having multi-billion-dollar companies as her competition, Sarah set about writing letters to local government and local councils to find grants. Within three months, she had secured several local government contracts.

Sarah ending up moving from the UK to Malta and thought her only option was to shut her business. She wasn't aware she could have sold her business. She closed the doors on her business and started another business in Malta. She adopted the same approach and contacted local government, establishing some key relationships in the business community. As a result, she secured some contracts with international hotel chains, the bank of Malta, and some key retailers.

Sarah's husband worked in the military, so another international move saw them move from Malta to Perth, Western Australia. Again, she adopted the same approach and within 18 months had built a seven-figure business with 23 employees and international training contracts. Nineteen months into her six-year contracts, she was told that the government funding was going to be pulled. When that funding was pulled, it gave her one of the hardest times of her life. With one phone call, she had 23 staff she couldn't pay, a six-figure tax bill she couldn't pay, and she was facing losing her house. She realised she had created her business on an unsustainable model.

Not one to shy away from a challenge, Sarah faced up to the situation and found another way of getting her expertise and her services out into the world. It was simple—online courses. She managed to get her courses up online, keep the tax man happy, and increase her revenue by 1900%. Instead of training people in one country, her online courses opened up her market to 121 countries. This resulted in her working flexible hours, and using 100% contractors, meaning her overheads dropped significantly and she has been able to outsource project-based tasks.

She is now living her definition of success: freedom, being able to work her own hours, working in a way she wants, and offering the value she wants to people.

Why is earning with online courses so great?

❖ **You create once**

Most of the work is upfront, once you have created the course, you can make money any time.

❖ **Passive income**

You can make money whilst you sleep, eat or vacation. An online course enables you to *create a recurring income* that comes in 24 hours a day.

❖ **Global reach**

> With online learning platforms such as Udemy and Thinkific, you are able to access a global audience. Being able to connect with people through the power of education makes you influential.

❖ **Scalability**

> When you run a bricks and mortar business such as a yoga studio, you are limited to how many people you can fit in each class as well as how many classes you can run. With an online course, you could teach yoga to unlimited students at no extra cost to you.

Sarah's tips on how to actually get started

1. Determine your topic

- Write down 100 things you know what to do, and give yourself a score out of 10 for each (ten being you have amazing knowledge and 1 being you've got little knowledge).
- Then write down 100 things you absolutely love. Give yourself a score out of 10 for each of them.
- Next write down 100 things you've experienced. Rate each experience out of 10.
- Put your three lists side by side. Where you've got a 10, 10, 10 across your lists, that's your perfect course topic.

2. Market research

- It's important to ensure there is *demand* for your course.

- If there are other courses on your topic, then that's great. Competition is a good thing.

3. Collect content

- Think about your course from your audience's point of view.
- What skills will they be practically able to demonstrate at the end of the course?
- What will they know at the end of the course?
- How will they feel at the end of the course?
- Gather all the data, facts, and information for your course. This can be done through a combination of methods such as internet research or brainstorming your knowledge.
- This is as much about what information to leave out as well as what needs to be included.
- Be careful to avoid information overload!

4. Map an outline

- Develop a list of topics or modules for your online course.
- Be conscious of the order of your topics/modules—each one should build on the previous topic/module or skill learnt and be logical for your audience to follow.

5. Record your content

- There are a number of ways to do this step. Think about how best to deliver the content such as videos, audio, reading, or activities.
- The most effective delivery method is video:

- o **Talking head video** – you are in shot on camera.
- o **Green screen** – you shoot the video with a giant green screen behind you. This allows you to have anything behind you in the editing phase such as PowerPoint slides or animation.
- o **Screencasting** – recording your computer screen.

6. Edit

- This phase will depend on your technical ability.
- Camtasia is software that allows you to edit videos yourself. It allows you to do a number of things such as add in logos, text, or fix the sound.
- Check out Sarah's YouTube "How to" on this here: https://www.youtube.com/watch?v=0pbkdmwtdro&feature=youtu.be

7. Set up on a platform

- There are three different ways to sell your online course, learning management systems (Thinkific or Udemy), online course marketplaces, or plugins or software on your website.

- Sarah advises, "A learning management system is your own Academy that you can link to your website and fully brand as your own platform. It makes online course creation simple and easy to sell your learning products."

The Cubicle Crusher's Hot Tip:

Lynda and Skillshare are a great resource for free and paid courses. Check them out to see what other courses are available in your chosen topic.

Sarah's tips on how to achieve the heights of success with online courses

1. Think about your ideal customer

Who are they? What language or key phrases do they use? How can you speak directly to them? How familiar is your customer with the topic? Speak directly to your customer.

2. Know what problem this will solve

People buy online courses because they have a problem and they need your help. What is your audience's greatest problem? *Be clear* on how this online course will solve their problem.

3. Focus on a completed outline before you get started

It's worth spending quality time on getting the outline right as it will directly relate to the success of your course. It's important to ensure your course delivers on its title. Think about the journey you are taking your audience on—does it flow? Will they be able to finish the course?

4. Develop inspiring content

How will your content inspire your audience to move through a pain point and transform? Your aim is to help your audience transform a part of their life in some way. It also helps to inject a bit of yourself into the course. This makes it relatable for your audience.

5. Create digestable, actionable learning modules

Break down your content in digestable chunks. Keep your content simple yet highly effective. Provide real-life examples to illustrate points. What actions will your audience need to complete along the way? For examples, quizzes, workbooks, or tasks.

6. Pricing

There is no right or wrong here, nor any pricing guideline for you. Online course prices can range anywhere from $47 to $9,997. Check out similar courses on your topic to understand the price point. Make sure your course is different and better. As long as your course is better, then you can price it slightly higher than others. According to Sarah, "Never price yours lower because that will just make yours look like it has less value than your competitors."

> *The Cubicle Crusher's Hot Tip:*
>
> *To price your course, check this out: https://www.learnworlds.com/course-revenue-calculator*

7. The launch

Once you've created your course, sales won't automatically start rolling in. You need to have a launch and *ongoing marketing strategy* in order to promote your course. Think about how you will promote it. There are a number of different ways such as early bird discounts, ads, promoting via social media, partnering up with influencers, or running an affiliate program. Sarah's advice is to "Remember that the second you stop marketing is the second you stop selling."

Where to find out more

You can connect with Sarah here:
- Website: www.sarahcordiner.com
- Facebook: www.facebook.com/cordinersarah/
- Twitter: www.twitter.com/cordinersarah/

Courses and websites:
- **Create Awesome Online Courses** by David Siteman Garland: This offers great tips and courses - https://www.createawesomeonlinecourses.com/
- **Video School Online**: This offers a huge list of online courses covering a broad range of topics - https://www.videoschoolonline.com/course-library
- **Social Triggers: How to create an online course** by Derek Halpern: This offers a free training on how to make money selling online courses - https://socialtriggers.com/courses/
- **The Udemy Course Creation & Marketing Blueprint** course by RW Studio: A small investment is

required for this one -
https://www.udemy.com/create-course-and-sell-online-udemy-courses/

- **Thinkific's Blog**: For all the inspiration and success stories from online course creators - http://blog.thinkific.com/category/success-stories/

<u>Chapter 6</u>

<u>Coaching</u>

"Recognising that you are not where you want to be is a starting point to begin changing your life." – Deborah Day

---

This chapter is for you if you have a passion for helping people and you enjoy seeing people make a meaningful change in their life.

*

According to the International Coaching Federation's latest Global Coaching Study, (Forbes), coaching is a booming industry, approximately a $2.5 billion a year industry with 53,000 professional coach practitioners worldwide. In the last ten years, it has grown exponentially and membership of the International Coaching Federation (ICF) has more than tripled. A 2016 report by the ICF noted the average hourly fee per coaching session was $120 USD per hour for a coach with less than one years' experience going up to $330 USD per hour for a coach with 10 years' experience. With hourly rates like these, you should **definitely** be considering coaching!

First of all, what is coaching? The ICF defines coaching as "partnering with clients in a thought-provoking and creative process that inspires them to maximise their personal and professional potential." Coaching operates in many different areas such as life, leadership, organisation, business, career, health, and wellness to name a few. The reasons why people see a coach are varied, however for individuals, it often includes overcoming challenges, lack of clarity in an area, or their life being out of balance.

So how much can you really make with a coaching business? The answer is it's up to you. Some inspirational success stories of coaches who have made over six figures include:

- Jessica Nazarali - Business Strategist and Certified Master Coach, (www.jessicanazarali.com)
- Stephanie Nickolich – Success Mentor "The Millionista Mentor" (www.stephanienickolich.com)
- Sarah Kaler – Business & Leadership Coach (www.sarahkaler.com)
- Kat Loterzo – Motivational Coach (www.katloterzo.com)
- Jamie Masters – Business Coach (www.eventualmillionaire.com)
- Andrew Ferebee - Personal development, success, dating and relationship coaching (www.knowledgeformen.com)
- Michael Serwa – Life Coach (www.michaelserwa.com)

One person who transitioned to being a success coach is Janelle Mason, who created her coaching company for aspiring female entrepreneurs. Janelle has built her success coaching company from the ground to six figures, creating a life she dreamed about and loves.

Janelle's Story

Born in Australia, Janelle graduated at 21 with a Bachelor of Law degree. She began her career practising law, fulfilling her childhood dream as she climbed the corporate ladder. After suffering a near fatal heart attack at 28, she was forced to reinvent herself. Her career was a key part of this and she worked in a number of different jobs before listening to her intuition and relocating to London.

Janelle took on different contract roles for a year until she came across a Facebook ad for a coach and her program. This coach seemed to be living a life they loved, and Janelle really wanted to love her life again. Despite not having any money, she was determined to complete the coaching program and used her emergency credit card to pay the first instalment of the course.

The six-month program was really life-changing for Janelle. Through mindset work, she learnt she had the **power to control her thoughts**, and as she applied her learning, she realised she had the ability to change her life. She started noticing changes in as early as two weeks into the program. Despite not having the second payment, she set up a registered limited company and opened a business bank account. Leveraging her network of high net worth individuals, Janelle managed to secure a three-month contract, using her law expertise to assist a Texas client who was facing insolvency. The earnings from her second invoice gave her the confidence to keep going.

Whilst building up her success coaching business, she was still contracting and freely admits to the fact there were definitely some 3am mornings as she was working a lot to build up her business. But over time, her success coaching business took off. She quickly developed a group program and in one week made $6K. She has continued that success and now operates a six-figure coaching business, loving and living life on her terms.

Why is coaching so great?

❖ **You are doing work aligned with your values**

As your values guide your choices in life, if you value helping people, then coaching is a rewarding and fulfilling career choice. When you are working in alignment with your values, you will feel more fulfilled.

❖ **You can start your business with low overheads**

Unlike other businesses, you don't need to make a large investment to establish your coaching business.

❖ **It helps you grow, develop, and evolve**

Your personal growth never ends, and as you coach your clients to fuel a profound and lasting personal and professional change, very often you will experience the same kind of transformation. The opportunity to learn off your clients only serves to enrich your development. In addition, undertaking your coaching qualification can really help to understand yourself.

❖ **You get to make a difference in people's lives**

Witnessing others transform and change their personal or professional life provides deep satisfaction and joy. Knowing you have supported someone through your coaching to a very satisfactory personal outcome is a *powerful motivator.*

❖ **It's a location-independent business**

With the ease of technology, it's never been easier to deliver coaching services via Skype or Facetime. This means you can work wherever you have an internet connection.

Janelle's tips on how to actually get started

1. **Experience coaching for yourself**

To be a great coach, it will help you immensely if you have experienced being coached. This will ensure you understand what it's like to be in your client's shoes. Once you have had first-hand experience of coaching and undertaken the journey of personal transformation, you will be more attractive to clients.

2. **Find a mentor**

Find an experienced coach who is where you want to be. This will help to push you outside *your comfort zone*, as well as give you the support, encouragement, guidance, and advice you need on your entrepreneur journey.

3. Get qualified

The coaching industry is unregulated, meaning anyone can call themselves a coach. If you are serious about becoming a coach, it is recommended to attain a qualification that is credentialed by the International Coaching Federation (ICF).

4. Clarify your niche of coaching

As the saying goes, *"The riches is in the niches"*. It's important to take the time to think about what specific area of coaching your business will focus on. Who is your ideal client? Why would you like to help them? What particular area will you focus on? Being clear on your niche will assist you to define your target market and structure your sales message to them.

5. Build a website

Potential clients need to learn about you and your offering. To ensure a strong online presence, get this established with some great content such as blog posts and testimonials if you have them.

The Cubicle Crusher's Hot Tip:

There's lots of coaches across the world. How are you different? Create your unique selling proposition (USP) to appeal to your target audience.

Janelle's tips on how to achieve the heights of success with coaching

1. Outsource as soon as you can

In order to build a coaching business, you need to be working **on** your business, not **in** your business. Ideally, you want to spend your time coaching or creating programs, not doing basic admin tasks. Outsourcing even simple tasks such as your social media is key to building a six- or seven-figure business.

2. Set up your business properly

Unlike other businesses, setting up a coaching business right from day one is important. It is advisable to get some legal and accounting advice. You will also need to get the terms and conditions up on your website as well as establishing a client contract. Knowing your business is set up correctly will protect you and give you confidence.

3. Get comfortable selling

In order to be a coach, you first need to be a salesperson. The most important part of business is making money; therefore you need to know how to sell your business and yourself.

4. Know your worth and charge it

It's essential that you're confident in yourself and your abilities and know how your skills will enable you to support your clients. You are selling your experience and expertise, so don't get caught charging lower prices—get your prices right from the beginning.

5. Sell group coaching

One-on-one coaching is great; however, in order to make six figures, group coaching **is** an important program you **need** to be offering. For example, say you charge $150 per hour for one-to-one coaching. You could charge $50 per hour for group coaching and make the same amount of money with three clients. Imagine getting 10, 15, or 25 group coaching clients. For the latter, that's $1,250 per hour—and you're working less.

> *The Cubicle Crusher's Hot Tip:*
>
> *Work with a coach who achieved the success you're after. They can help you fast-track your success.*

Where to find out more

You can connect with Janelle here:
- Website: www.janellemason.com
- Facebook: www.facebook.com/JanelleMason.Success.Coach/
- Instagram: www.instagram.com/janelle_mason_/

Courses and websites:

- There are many different coaching courses available—check out the ICF website for more information: www.coachfederation.org

<u>Chapter 7</u>

<u>Blogging</u>

"Starting something new or making a big change requires effort, persistence and motivation. Doubt, fear & worry will only slow you down. Focus on doing your best now & celebrate every step of the way." – Doe Zantamata

---

This chapter is for those people who love writing, want a creative outlet, aren't afraid to share their views with the world, and want to share their views through a blog.

*

In recent years, blogging has become an incredibly popular way to earn income, create a business, and sell products you have created. According to Natasha Courtenay-Smith of The Million Dollar Blog, "Blogging has become the "it" career of the modern world". There are 2.7 million blog posts published every day. Over 409 million people view more than 23.8 billion pages each month.

But before we go any further, you might be wondering, what is a blog? Blog Inc. describes blogs as being "an interactive website that delivers regular content to its readers". So, what makes a great blog? You probably have your own version of what a blog is, but it's like a good pizza—there's different variations for everyone. There are blogs on every topic from fashion to lifestyle, food to business. Name any topic and there's probably a blog about it.

Blogging can provide you with a way to **crush the cubicle**. With a little as a laptop, an email address, and an internet connection, you can get started on your way to blogging success. There are many examples of people who have replaced their 9 to 5 job with the income earned from their blog, including:

- Pat Flynn: Earns over $100K per month - www.smartpassiveincome.com
- Michelle Schroeder-Gardner: Earns over $130K per month – www.makingsenseofcents.com
- Abby Lawson: Earns over $30K per month – www.justagirlandherblog.com
- Darren Rowse: Earns over $40K per month – www.problogger.com
- Elsie Larson and Emma Chapman: Earns $1.5 million per year – www.abeautifulmess.com

There are *a number* of ways for a blog to earn money, however earnings can be grouped into two areas: **direct and indirect earnings**. Direct earnings come from helping to sell other companies' products or your own products and advertising. Indirect earnings come from opportunities that arise as a result of your blog's success.

<u>Direct earnings:</u>

- Advertising or banner ads
- Affiliate marketing
- Digital products
- Blog post sponsorship deals
- Branded products

<u>Indirect earnings:</u>

- Coaching or consulting
- Freelance blogging
- Apps
- Speaking and book deals
- Writing for magazine and television presenting

The Cubicle Crusher's Hot Tip:

Don't get fixated on one income source. During your blogging journey, different income sources will appeal more than others.

One person who started a blog that enabled her to **crush the cubicle** is Kate McKibbin of the blogs **Drop Dead Gorgeous Daily** and **Secret Bloggers Business**.

Kate's Story

Kate started out working in publishing and worked for an Australian magazine called *Shop Till You Drop*. With long hours and low pay, she started her blog Drop Dead Gorgeous Daily. She called it her "Shoe Money Project", and started the blog as a way to give her extra income to buy Jimmy Choo shoes instead of Target shoes. This was back in 2007 when the world of online shopping was starting to take off. She came up with an idea that she wanted to highlight different fashion stores to people, educate people in the world of online shopping, as well as highlight that whilst things might be full priced in Australia, you could shop and ship things internationally at half the price.

As Kate had identified a spot in a market that was really taking off, her blog grew quite quickly. After 12 months, she was able to say goodbye to her nine to five, earning enough money via advertising and affiliate marketing.

When Kate started her blog, she had absolutely no idea what she was doing. Today, her blog has over 450,000 plus readers a month with a multiple six figure revenue and five staff. Over her blogging journey, Kate has created her own collection of nail polishes with Revlon, sat front row at New York Fashion Week, and been named one of Anthill's 30 Under 30 Entrepreneurs.

She kept getting asked again and again how she turned her little shoe money side project into an amazingly rewarding and profitable business. It was exactly that—Kate treated her blog like a business. Three years ago, she decided to start Secret Bloggers Business to teach others and be able to help them grow their blog quicker and faster. After all, she'd spent so much time working it out that she was able to help people over the hardest part of their blogging journey—getting started. So she turned her biggest blogging and business lessons into three different online courses for bloggers.

Why is blogging so great?

❖ **You get to share your passion with others**

If you have a hobby or interest that you are *deeply passionate* about, blogging is a great way to connect with others who have a similar interest. Maybe you're a movie buff or committed Formula 1 fan—blogging offers you a place to share your knowledge. It's also easier to motivate yourself when you do something from a place of intense passion.

❖ **You can crush the cubicle and escape your nine to five**

Blogging has great potential to generate income for you. There are many bloggers who make all their money from their blog. There are many ways to earn income from your blog. How quickly you earn income from your blog will depend on you and your goals.

❖ **You can get started very cheaply**

In the process of setting up your business, it doesn't get much easier than starting a blog. There's no huge upfront investment to get your blog up and running. In fact, you can set your blog up on WordPress, which is free to use, highly secure, and customisable.

❖ **You can build a community**

Blogging is a great way to attract readers and build a network. Through sharing your views and interests, readers will get to know you and in turn offer their feedback, which leads to conversation. This conversation connects people and puts you in contact with a wide variety of people, some of which may become lifelong friends.

❖ **You can build your profile**

A blog helps to demonstrate your knowledge and increases your chances of getting noticed. It helps you to develop and *build your personal brand* and raise your profile within your business market or community. A raised profile can open up opportunities you may never have thought of.

Kate's tips on how to actually get started

1. **Get crystal clear on why you are starting your blog**

You are starting this blog to make money, create a lifestyle around your passion, set your own hours, and live a more balanced lifestyle. Getting crystal clear on your why is really important as it will give you the energy and inspiration to keep you going.

2. **Decide what you will blog about**

It's important to be clear on what the purpose of your blog is. This is one of the most essential decisions you will make when building your blog. Take a blank piece of paper, sit somewhere free from distractions, and write down your answers to these questions:

- What is your ideal reader or target audience?
- What problem does your ideal reader or target audience have?
- What does your ideal reader or target audience want to know?

3. Define your niche

Many bloggers start out by creating a personal blog. These blogs cover a wide range of topics and interests such as personal views, experiences, and life in general. They can also be an extension of the blogger's life. As you are starting this blog as a business, it is important to define your niche.

The majority of profitable blogs have a defined niche. A niche is a very defined, specific segment of the market. For example, career coaching for women over 40.

Darren Rowse of Problogger says, "Blogging consistently on one single topic increases the chances of that blog (and its blogger) being seen as a credible, trusted source of information in that area. Work this correctly and you can become the "go-to" person in your niche and become known as a specialist or expert in your field."

4. Choose a name for your blog

As well as choosing a name closely linked to your content, it *needs* to be memorable. Something that is easy for people to remember and not too long or with any complicated words. Keep in mind that it should be *simple* and *straightforward* for your readers to locate your blog in a search engine.

Check your blog name is available by typing it into a search engine.

5.   Setting up your blog

Unless you are a technical guru, it's best to use one of the online blogging platforms, also called **blog software**, to help you set up your blog.

Whilst there are many blog platforms available, WordPress is the most popular open source blogging software available. Go to www.wordpress.org to download this. There are tutorials on the site to help you get started.

6.   Select your own domain name

You will need to buy your own domain name, not the one that comes with the blog platform you are using. The reason for this is you want to build credibility and professionalism around your blog. For example, www.thecubiclecrusher.com is my domain name rather than www.thecubiclecrusher.wordpress.org. This also gives you the ability to have your own email address instead of a Hotmail or Gmail address. This adds to the professionalism of your blog.

Buying your own domain name isn't too complicated. Go to a **web hosting site** such as www.godaddy.com and for around $10 to $30 per year, you can purchase your domain name if it's available. If it's not available, it's being used by someone else, so spend time brainstorming other relevant names.

> **The Cubicle Crusher's Hot Tip:**
>
> *In order to build your blog, it's so important to build momentum by taking massive action. Also network like crazy to build up a group of people that know you and know what your blog is about.*

Kate's tips on how to achieve the heights of success with blogging

1. Business Mindset

From day one, approach your blog with *a business mindset*, not like a hobby. This means thinking commercially about how you are going to make money from your blog. It's vital to know this from the start and have a plan for monetisation, as there's a staggering 15 different methods you could choose from. These include ads, eBooks, coaching, workshops, physical products, events, digital downloads, or teaching. It's about finding the right mix and what works for you as well as what works for your topic, your readers, and what you're happy to do.

You are your business' greatest asset, so make sure you always have the best information to share, the best systems and tools available, and think about it from a place of true commercial terms.

2. Value Your Time

If you are building your blog whilst working full time, then it's about using what time you have wisely. Set aside time in 30-, 45-, or 60-minute blocks. Write a list of all the tasks that need to be done for your blog such as writing blog posts, posting to social media, reading and commenting on other blogs, or blog maintenance. Allocate certain times throughout the week to a set task. For example, you might find two x 60-minute blocks on the weekend to write several blog posts for the upcoming week and then allocate 30 minutes a few days later to schedule and post them.

Alternatively, it may be that you **outsource** some of your tasks by hiring a virtual assistant. Check out www.upwork.com to find a suitable virtual assistant. This can be a great use of your time and money, as this investment allows you spend time on other activities such as planning.

3. Traffic

There's no certain level of traffic you need in order to start monetising your blog, although a few thousand visitors per month is ideal to start with, while anything over that is a bonus. It's more about having a greater chance of converting your readers to customers. Kate's blog, Drop Dead Gorgeous Daily has 500,000 plus visitors per month, compared with her other blog Secret Bloggers Business, which in its best month had 20,000 visitors. However, Secret Bloggers Business was far more profitable due to the number of readers who ended up purchasing something.

4. Learn along the way

Be prepared to try new things. This means you are always learning and upskilling. As you try different things, you will be able to see what works and what doesn't and then make tweaks along the way.

5. Consistency is key

Be consistent with the tone and schedule of your writing. You need to publish content regularly such as weekly, bi-weekly, or daily, as this will assist your audience in getting to know you and your blog. It will also ensure they return and become regular readers.

Where to find out more

You can connect with Kate here:
- Website: www.secretbloggersbusiness.com
- Facebook: www.facebook.com/secretbloggersbusiness
- Instagram: www.instagram.com/secretbloggersbusiness

Books
- *The Million Dollar Blog* – Natasha Courtenay-Smith
- *Blog Inc* – Joy Deangdeelert Cho
- *Born to Blog* – Mark W. Schaefer and Stanford A. Smith
- *Problogger* – Darren Rowse and Chris Garrett

Websites

- www.problogger.com
- www.wpbeginner.com
- www.bloggingbasics101.com
- www.secretbloggersbusiness.com

Chapter 8

eCommerce, Part 1: eBay

---

*"Think big and don't listen to people who tell you it
can't be done. Life's too short to think small."* –
Tim Ferris

This chapter is for those who don't want to invest a lot of
money upfront to start their business or worry about sourcing
and driving traffic and who enjoy selling.

*

eBay is essentially a multinational eCommerce company with a
presence in more than 33 markets. Its primary business is a
shopping website and auction platform through which people
and businesses can buy and sell a large variety of products and
services worldwide. To put it simply, eBay is a marketplace that
purely connects sellers with buyers.

Originally called AuctionWeb, eBay was launched during the
U.S. Labor Day weekend in 1995 by entrepreneur Pierre
Omidyar from his living room in San Jose, California. The first
ever item to sell on eBay was a used, broken laser pointer. As

of October 2016, there are 165 million users of eBay. Some of the eBay success stories include:

- Ben Doyle – makes over $20,000 per month on eBay selling fashion and furniture
- Linda Lightman – makes $25 million a year on eBay selling fashion via her luxury consignment store **Linda's Stuff**
- Scott Gladstone – makes over $8 million a year on eBay selling exercise gear via his e-tail store **Klika**
- Corri McFadden – founded **eDrop-Off**, which resells designer clothes on eBay – is an eBay millionaire
- Paul Nieuwenhuys – of eBay store **Hooked, Online and Sinker** makes more than $1 million each year selling fishing tackle
- Michael Dash – eBay Platinum Seller makes over $6 million each year selling auto parts via **Car Parts Kings**

One of the **world's leading eBay educators** is Amanda Clarkson. Together with her husband, she is a self-made eBay millionaire. Amanda has built a very successful eBay business and has been sharing her knowledge of selling online to students all over the world since 2006.

Amanda's Story

Amanda says she always had an interest in living a fulfilled life, even from a very young age. She recalls how even as a 4-year old she was interested in making money and 'getting rich'. As a child, she would do all sorts of things to earn money, selling fruit to the neighbours, cooking cupcakes and cookies to sell, even having a lolly stand. One of five kids, school wasn't really for Amanda. She found school incredibly difficult, failing every single subject except religion and art. At age 16, armed with nothing more than a burning desire to go out and make something of her life, she left school.

The road after school wasn't necessarily super smooth for Amanda, even though her desire for success was strong. She had 33 jobs in a 10-year period and absolutely hated every single job that she had. She would wake up each morning not wanting to go to work and it really felt like something was missing. She wasn't feeling fulfilled, nor was she happy.

Amanda started to venture into different bricks and mortar businesses from the beauty industry to video shops, real estate, a food van, and personal training. As Amanda says, "You name it, I've done it". An honest conversation with her husband Matt back in 2006 confirmed they were both disgruntled with their life, and fed up with getting up each morning doing the same thing but hoping for a different result.

One afternoon whilst walking along the beach, Matt was whinging about his persistent sore back from his work as a carpenter. Matt said to Amanda, "I just can't keep doing this", she turned to him and said, "For God's sake, do something about it!" After the two of them recovered from the shock of her blunt and direct comment, it was then that they started on the search for a better lifestyle. One that would give them a life they truly felt inspired by and absolutely loved. Their search to find something on the internet began.

It was in the early 2000s when the internet was just coming into fashion, and Amanda admits she'd never sent an email, but she did have an open mind when Matt said to her, "I know that people make money on the internet". They dived deeply into the internet, even travelling to Nashville, Tennessee, for their very first internet seminar. They both fell in love with the idea of having an internet business. They knew people were making money on the internet, but they didn't know how.

Three years into their journey, they still hadn't made any money. In fact, they had lost money simply from investing in courses, trying everything, and giving it a go. Determined not to quit, they kept going, quietly confident that something will happen.

One day whilst sitting in their office, Matt got an email about eBay and he said to Amanda, "Oh, this looks interesting. Why don't you check it out?" So Amanda did. She started looking at eBay and felt her heart rate go up, and she noticed herself getting really excited about this website. She could see that people would exchange products for money, which made sense to her. After doing a lot of research, she found out that all she had to do to make money was to fill a need in the market. Simply put—connect people with products.

What really appealed to Amanda about eBay, aside from it being online shopping, was that she didn't need to build a website, didn't need to find traffic as eBay gave you all the traffic you could handle, and probably the biggest drawcard of all, she didn't need experience. So with all of their boxes ticked, Amanda and Matt set out on their eBay journey.

They started a business importing health and fitness products. Whilst waiting for their first shipment to arrive, Amanda started selling anything around the house, making about $700 net profit a week whilst learning the ropes. Once the shipment arrived, they put the products up on eBay and within six months were turning over $60,000 AUD to $75,000 AUD per month.

Amanda is still as passionate today as she was back in 2006, joking that eBay is her "second boyfriend".

Why is eBay so great?

❖ **People come to eBay wanting to buy**

As eBay is a shopping website and auction platform, people have their credit card ready to purchase.

❖ **You can start today**

Take a look at what you have lying around your house. Any items you no longer need or use are the first products that you can sell.

You don't need to have any experience or particular expertise in eBay or online business. The great thing about eBay is you can learn as you go.

❖ **You can get started on almost any budget**

There's no upfront costs or investment to start selling. If you start with selling unwanted items from around your house, you can re-invest the cash you have earnt into purchasing other items to sell.

❖ **It's a safe and smart business option**

With any business, you need a website and traffic coming to your site, which you convert into customers. With eBay, there's no need to build a website or find traffic as there is already a steady stream of traffic coming to eBay every day.

❖ It's a business you can automate

Whilst eBay is absolutely a business, once you are up and running, you can automate over 90% of the processes.

> *The Cubicle Crusher's Hot Tip:*
>
> *Want to read more about becoming an eBay millionaire? Buy Matt & Amanda Clarkson's eBook "1001 eBay Success Secrets"*

Amanda's tips on how to actually get started on eBay

1. Open an eBay account

To get started selling on eBay, you will need to set up an account. It's the same kind of account that eBay shoppers use and it's free. You can set up a personal or business account. Remember if you set up a business account, you will need to have your business set up legally and correctly.

2. Choose your ID

You will need to choose a seller ID. User56948 is hardly inspiring or attractive to potential customers. Think about your branding and choose a name that your customers will identify with.

3.　Make some purchases

Make a few purchases yourself to understand how eBay shopping works. Before you can sell on eBay, you need to understand how people on eBay buy. It's also important you have an eBay history and a good buyer rating. Ensure you pay for your goods promptly and provide customer feedback.

4.　Start small

Start out selling one or two things from around the house.

5.　Find your niche market

With *over 50,000 categories* on eBay, it's easy to get overwhelmed and want to sell goods in several. Pick one category or niche market that you are interested in and work at becoming an expert at that. Understand what the buyers of that niche look for in purchasing products. Look on the wider internet to understand who else sells products in this niche category. Know everything there is to know about your niche.

6.　Research

Have a look at other sellers on eBay—how are they marketing their products? Use the 'most popular' tool on eBay to find out what the hottest items are at a particular time. Check out which items have the *most bids* on them or what the *most watched items* are. Similarly, look at what items aren't getting many or any bids. This will help you to understand what will sell and what won't.

7. Sell new stuff

81% of things sold on eBay are brand new. Try searching retail or shop outlets for products you can buy. You'll be able to buy things at a fraction of the price they retail for.

Amanda's tips on how to achieve the heights of success with eBay

1. eBay is a search engine

eBay is like Google as it's run on search algorithms. This means that when you are selling a product, you need to make sure you have *specific keywords* in the title description. There's room for a specific number of characters, so it's important to use words that people are actually searching for.

2. Have incredible photos

You know the saying, "A picture is worth a thousand words". It's no different on eBay. In fact, it's even more important on eBay because the seller can't actually touch or feel the product they're visually seeing. Therefore, you need to ensure your photo shows the product from all different angles. There's no need to spend a fortune on a camera you probably can't afford. Use your smartphone and ensure the lighting is good, and there is a clear white background with no junk or anything else that might get in the way of a great photo.

3. People love stories

This is really about tapping into a bit of buyer psychology. Too many sellers point out the features of the product, but people aren't buying the features. They want to *buy the benefits* of the product. For example, if you were selling jeans, you would point out that they make you look trim and slim, they take inches off your waist, and make you look five centimetres taller, rather than saying they are blue jeans with studs on the pockets. This will help you draw people into wanting to buy that product and will ultimately help you to be a more successful seller.

4. Treat it like a business

You *need* to have a business mindset about your eBay selling, not a hobby mindset. This means ensuring you are making money, recording expenses, getting great customer feedback, and committed to succeeding.

5. Perfect pricing

Don't simply put a price on your product and off you go. Have a look at what other sellers have sold similar items for. Don't be the cheapest. People don't buy on price alone, as 75% of the buyers go to eBay for experience and value. People who are on the internet are very mature and sophisticated with their purchasing these days. Think about the value of the product and experience buying the product will give your customer. Think about how you can offer something that other sellers don't. Put yourself in the customer's shoes.

It's also essential that you understand eBay's pricing structure as you will be charged a fee for each item that you sell. Do your research so there's no surprises.

The Cubicle Crusher's Hot Tip:

Think like a buyer!

Where to find out more

You can connect with Amanda here:

- Website: www.livenoweducation.com
- Facebook: www.facebook.com/livenowtvcom/
- Instagram: www.instagram.com/livenowedu

Courses and websites:

- **"The Live Now Freedom Formula: The Secret to Living a Life that you love with Multiple Income Streams that lets you have it all"** course by Amanda Clarkson. This was developed from over 30 years of mistakes and learnings, plus has lots of great tips to help get you started. To get your *free* gift, worth a huge $497, go to - www.livenoweducation.com/jenny

eBay has lots of information to assist you:

- Getting started - http://pages.ebay.com/help/account/gettingstarted.html

- Questions - http://pages.ebay.com.au/help/sell/questions/list-item.html

- Learn to sell online - http://pages.ebay.com/seller-center/new-to-ebay/learn-to-sell-online.html

- Seller Center - http://pages.ebay.com/seller-center/index.html

A simple search in Google will provide you with lots of information to help you on your eBay journey.

Chapter 9

eCommerce, Part 2: Online Stores & Amazon

"If you think that you are going to love something, give it a try. You're going to kick yourself in the butt for the rest of your life, if you don't." – Joe Penna

This chapter is for those who want to leverage a huge marketplace, are happy to source products, and don't won't to do too much after that. If you're focused on building brand equity for yourself and have a complete understanding of your customer, such as who they are and how much they have brought, then this chapter is also for you.

*

Let's face it, online shopping has grown exponentially. You only have to look at the number of your favourite retailers who have an online presence as well as a traditional bricks and mortar business. Its popularity has grown to the point where many businesses, such as Amazon, sell online only. As consumers, this suits us and our busy, fast-paced, and hectic lifestyle. We love the convenience of being able to shop whenever we want, source products, and access bargains from across the world.

With the increase in online shopping, there has never been a better time to start an eCommerce business. Ecommerce is the transaction of buying and selling online. You can see the rapid rise in the volume of eCommerce purchases:

- More than 80% of the online population has used the internet to make a purchase.
- The top 10 retail eCommerce countries based on current size and future potential are, in order, USA, China, UK, Japan, Germany, France, South Korea, Russia, Belgium, and Australia.
- People between 18 and 35 do the most online research via mobile devices.
- Consumers are doing more than 50% of their shopping online.
- 55% of shoppers said customer reviews affect their buying decisions.
- The U.S. leads in overall eCommerce spending.
- The Asian-Pacific nations lead Business to Consumer Sales (B2C) with an expected $707 billion plus of sales in 2017.
- By 2018, global retail eCommerce sales are expected to approach $2.5 trillion.

The growth in this space means there is *high demand* for products and a wealth of opportunities. The online business models of Amazon as well as the vast array of ecommerce site builders such as Shopify and BigCommerce, have created a simple way to get an online store up and running in no time.

Through targeted pricing, identifying a niche, and sourcing quality product, anyone can **make an income that replaces their 9 to 5**.

e-Commerce success stories include:

- **Sophie Amoruso**: Sold vintage clothing – www.nastygirl.com
- **Andy Dunn**: Sells men's clothing and accessories – www.bonobos.com
- **Jake Nickell**: A creative community that makes, supports and buys great art – www.threadless.com
- **Susan and Eric Koger**: Sells fashionable vintage must-haves for women – www.modcloth.com
- **Katia Beauchamp**: A beauty box subscription for women - www.birchbox.com
- **Irwin Dominguez**: Who started a dropshipping business and went from zero to $1 million in sales in 8 months. Read about his story here - https://au.oberlo.com/blog/first-time-ecommerce-entrepreneur-story/

To understand the world of eCommerce further, I chatted with Steve Chou and Ken Eu. Steve created an online store, Bumblebee Linens, to replace his wife's salary and allow her to stay at home whilst raising their children. Steve has also gone on to create "The Sellers Summit", the ultimate eCommerce learning conference. Ken is a successful Amazon FBA seller who has replaced his income and now mentors others to do the same.

Steve's Story

It was 2007 and according to Steve, he and his wife were *victims* of a condition they called *complacency*. Put very simply, this is a disease where the person spends up to 10 hours or more at a job they don't particularly like. Whilst they both made decent salaries from their jobs, they felt like they were coasting through life.

Their typical day involved working from 9am to 6.30pm, eating dinner, and watching TV until it was time to go to bed. Steve suddenly got an injection of motivation and enthusiasm when his wife became pregnant with their first child. He felt he needed to get his act together and build a strong financial future for his family. Steve's wife wanted to be able to care for her child full time without the pressure of having to work a job, however she didn't want to have to change their lifestyle as a result. It was simple—they needed to find another way to make money and replace her six-figure salary.

Steve and his wife initially got started on eBay. They were looking for handkerchiefs for their upcoming wedding (primarily because his wife knew she was going to cry at the altar) and they couldn't find any locally. After some research, they located a place in China and due to a minimum order number, had to buy a heap of them. They only used a handful and then sold the rest on eBay. They ended up selling really quickly and their online store idea was born.

Ironically, once they had sold off the excess handkerchiefs on eBay, they did not pursue the eCommerce world for another two or three years. However, when they did start their business, their first six months were pretty miserable. The sales just weren't coming in a quickly as they would have liked.

After running some ads, doing a lot of marketing and understanding how search engines rank, things started to improve for Steve. His efforts started to pay off and they started to see sales coming in, replacing his wife's salary of $100K within a year. Their success attracted others who were interested in learning how Steve started his business, so he began documenting it on his blog, "My Wife Quit Her Job". He simply detailed all the steps that he took to grow the business. He also put out articles and posts related to having an e-commerce store. As a result, people began to look upon Steve as an authority on eCommerce. Now, as well as his business and blog, he also teaches a course, has a podcast, and runs an eCommerce conference once a year.

> *The Cubicle Crusher's Hot Tip:*
>
> *Want to hear more from Steve? Check out the "My Wife Quit Her Job Podcast" where he interviews small business entrepreneurs who are killing it online.*

Ken's Story

After graduating in Health Science and being unsure what to do with his degree, Ken decided to become a personal trainer. With a clientele that included CEOs, directors, and entrepreneurs, his mind began opening to the possibility of a different life. A life that was more than the 9 to 5 job.

Ken's clients advised him that if you want to be rich or successful, then you need to start your own business and selling is a big part of that success. Through the art of selling, a business will thrive—not just survive. In order to attain these skills, he obtained a job in sales and also started an online teaching platform on the side. The online teaching platform provided him with a big learning experience, although it took a lot of his time and money for very little success.

Down to his last $2,200 AUD in savings, Ken was wondering what else he could do online. He started looking on YouTube at different ways to make money online. He stumbled across one video about people making money on Amazon. After watching a few more videos and reading a few blogs, he decided to give selling on Amazon a go. He spent $1,000 AUD on products in China, which he then shipped to Amazon to sell, although it didn't quite turn out as he hoped—failing to turn a profit.

Still believing Amazon was a viable opportunity, he set about doing research and even paid for some courses on how to sell on Amazon. With $500 USD, he brought a few items from Walmart, a pram for about $50 USD, a few gym balls, a few nerf guns, a few toys, and some Xbox games. Equipped with everything he had learnt, he sent them to Amazon. Within two days of the shipment going to Amazon, Ken sold the pram for $150 USD. After the Amazon and administration fees came out, Ken realised he made $75 USD.

Thinking this was pretty good considering he'd made a profit whilst he was asleep, Ken continued with this model of buying cheaply and selling for a profit. So he continued shopping at his list of 150 retailers for things on special, clearance sales, or buy one get one free. He found the constant online searching for bargains very time-consuming and decided to hire help in the form of a staff member from an outsourcing website. Their primary job was to find products for Ken to sell. He initially started off buying five to ten units of products, although this increased over time to buying pallets of products, which he then sent on to Amazon.

About seven months into it, Ken realised he had enough capital to do something called private label. This involves finding a niche in the Amazon marketplace where there is not a lot of product offerings, via a website such as www.alibaba.com. You source the products cheaply, stick your own label on them, and launch them on Amazon.

By pricing appropriately and with effective marketing, Ken managed to bring in sales that replaced his full-time income about six months into his selling journey. Interestingly, he still does personal training, not for the money, but because one of his clients has been an amazing mentor to him and a massive help on the business side of things.

Ken has his Amazon business so streamlined that it only takes four to six hours of his time a week, that's it! Not a bad business and lifestyle. Ken's story shows the power of *surrounding yourself with like-minded people.*

Why is eCommerce so great?

❖ **24/7**

Unlike the traditional bricks and mortar business where you have fixed opening hours, an eCommerce business can operate 24/7. This allows you to take advantage of consumers who are shopping at all different hours of the day and earn money whilst you sleep.

❖ Global reach

An eCommerce business opens you up to a global audience. This expands the opportunities for selling your products and enables greater revenue to be earned.

❖ Low overheads

No rent to pay, no landlord to contend with, no shop to fit out with fixtures and furnishings, limited staff or the ability to hire staff from wherever around the world, no need to pay insurance, no huge electricity bills. This makes an e-commerce store very attractive. All you need is a computer and an internet connection.

❖ Automated

An eCommerce store can be automated through the streamlining of processes or the use of software. That enables you to be working or doing other things such as enjoying your life, going to the movies, going to the beach, or going out for coffee.

❖ Consumers are buying more online than in store

According to a survey by comScore and UPS, shoppers now make 51% of their purchases online. Additionally, the use of smartphones to make purchases has also increased. The survey showed that 44% of smartphone users are making purchases through their device compared with 41% the year before.

Steve's tips on how to actually get started with an eCommerce store

1. Decide what to sell

Know the products that you would like to sell online. It's important to choose a product that you understand and are passionate about. Survey friends and family by asking them some questions:

- What are you buying online right now?
- What products have you found difficult to find or source?
- Is there something you can buy that will help you out in your situation?

2. Validate your products or niche

Test whether your products or niche is actually going to sell. Check out top selling products on Amazon or eBay to understand what people are buying and confirm whether there is demand. With an already established marketplace, Amazon and eBay will bring traffic to your products. It's also useful to have a look in the news to uncover unmet needs or products already in demand.

3. Find a vendor

How would you obtain the products you have settled on? Your best bet in terms of margins is to have it manufactured yourself by a vendor, preferably somewhere overseas where the labour costs are a lot cheaper.

You can read more about vendor options on Steve's website: http://mywifequitherjob.com/the-best-way-to-find-vendors-for-your-online-store/

4. Establish a website

It's essential that you have an attractive and findable website for your eCommerce store. This enables your customers to find your product, and learn more about your product and about you. Once you have your own website, then you can start gathering email addresses and running ads, which opens up a whole lot of avenues for traffic.

5. Position your product

No matter what you choose to sell, you *need* to find some sort of *unique value proposition*. That is, the "something" that sets you apart from others. Have a look at your competitors and decide how your product is different. Also think what would keep your customers coming back. It could be your service or your value. For example, the unique value proposition for Bumblebee Linens is having the largest selection of handkerchiefs online. They also personalise them in-house, which enables the turnaround time to be one or two days.

The Cubicle Crusher's Hot Tip:

Did you know that you can use PayPal for your online research and to find what people are buying the most?

Ken's tips on how to actually get started with an Amazon business

1. Get the basics right

You will need to have an Amazon Seller Account to get started. There is a free or paid account, so make sure you know which one you're getting.

Before you start selling, you will need a computer, the internet, a smartphone, a printer, labels, boxes, shipping tape, and a weighing scale.

2. Understand Amazon's processes

As you are partnering with Amazon, you have to play by their rules. They are allowing you to sell on their platform, so it's important you know what's happening on Amazon. Make sure you understand exactly how selling on Amazon works. Be clear on which part you as the seller will handle and which part Amazon will handle. You can access the rules through the "Help" section on Amazon.

3. Start with Retail Arbitrage

Retail Arbitrage is buying products from retail stores either online or locally and then reselling those products on Amazon. The goal is to find products that you can sell on Amazon for a profit after you have paid for the item and Amazon has taken its fee, which is a percentage of the selling price.

4. Start small

Instead of buying huge quantities of product, start with smaller numbers. For example, buy five or 10 units rather than 100. Once you have sold them, you can buy more.

It's also important to think about the size of your product as this will affect the shipping cost. Smaller products are cheaper to ship.

5. Package and label with care

Whilst you need to find and source the product, you will also need to prepare and ship the product to Amazon's warehouse. It's no good having done all that work sending the product to Amazon for it to be damaged along the way. Make sure you have enough packing in your shipment so if something does happen to the box, such as it being dropped, your product will still be okay.

Ken and Steve's tips on how to achieve the heights of success with an eCommerce business or Amazon store

1. Know your numbers

You *need* to know your numbers in order to grow your business. Your numbers will tell you how healthy your business is and give you the foundation to grow. Understanding your numbers helps you to *measure success* and make better decisions. Some of the key metrics to review are:

- Average daily / monthly sales
- Average order value
- Average number of visits before purchase
- Revenue per visit

2. Use Alibaba to source products

One of the best ways to source products is through a site called www.alibaba.com. It is the leading platform for global wholesale trade. They have hundreds of millions of products in over 40 different categories. Whether it's sourcing the product or contacting a supplier in their local language, this site is valuable for your business needs. Regardless of what product you are after, Alibaba will present you with a list of suppliers.

3. Use the Amazon FBA program

The Fulfillment by Amazon (FBA) program is ideal for anyone who wants to start selling on Amazon. Whilst you are responsible for finding products you want to sell on Amazon, listing them, and preparing them to sell, once the products are listed and ready for sale, Amazon does the rest. When your product is sold, Amazon will find the box, schedule the shipment, pack the item, and make sure it gets to the buyer on time.

4. Get passionate about your customer

Keep your customer *centre* and *front* of everything you do. They are your greatest asset, so it's important to ensure they have a good experience buying your product. Collect and share testimonials and reviews to encourage more sales as this builds trust and confidence in your products. Remember, what your customers say about your product or business will ultimately have the *greatest impact* on buying decisions.

Where to find out more

You can connect with Steve here:
- Website: www.mywifequitherjob.com
- Facebook: www.facebook.com/mywifequitherjob
- Twitter: www.twitter.com/mywifequit

You can connect with Ken here:
- Facebook: www.facebook.com/kennetheucoaching/

Courses:
- **"How to Create A Niche Online Store in 5 Easy Steps"** course by Steve Chou. Jump on to Steve's

website www.mywifequitherjob.com and enter your details to access his free course.

- **"Create a Profitable Online Store"** course by Steve Chou. In this course, Steve breaks down the exact steps he took to earn $100K in the span of a year with his online shop - http://profitableonlinestore.com/special/course-signup/?ap_id=ecommercefuel

Conference:

- **"The Ultimate Ecommerce Learning Conference"** is organised and run by Steve Chou. Get inspired by success stories and get all the knowledge you need to run a successful eCommerce business – www.sellerssummit.com

Chapter 10

Podcasting

> "How can you squander even one more day not taking advantage of the greatest shifts of our generation? How dare you settle for less when the world has made it so easy for you to be remarkable?" – Seth Godin

This chapter is for people who love to connect with others and are comfortable using their voice to create that connection.

*

As consumers, our appetite for podcasts has increased as they become the new radio, and consequently our medium of choice. Listening to them has never been so easy, with 64% of podcasts being listened to on a smartphone or tablet. We're able to consume them in virtually any computer-free environment such as our car or at the gym.

According to the statistics, podcast listeners get hooked. Those in the UK listen to over 6 hours per week and those in Australia listen to 5.5 hours per week. In the U.S., with only 21% of the population are listening monthly, there's still plenty of opportunity to convert the rest.

So what are podcasts? A podcast is "a digital audio or video file or recording, usually part of a themed series, that can be downloaded from a website to a media player or computer" (www.dictionary.com).

Podcasts can be about any topic that people are interested in or passionate about and most are free to download and listen to. You simply subscribe to a podcast via iTunes or an app on your phone to have each episode automatically downloaded when it is released.

From a business perspective, podcasts are a great way to share your voice, gain an audience, and build your brand. There are a number of ways that podcasts can be profitable.

- **Sponsorships** – This is the most common way to *monetise* a podcast. Popular podcasts such as *Entrepreneur on Fire*, *The $100 MBA Show*, and *The Art of Charm* generate thousands of dollars per month in sponsorship dollars. You will need to have a very popular podcast with lots of downloads in order to generate significant revenue. The amount you receive will be a result of how many downloads you get. This is called cost per impression or CPM. For example, for 1,000 downloads of your show, you would earn $18 for a 15 second pre-roll.

- **Affiliate marketing** – As with this approach, you are marketing someone else's product for them. Pat Flynn of the Smart Passive Income podcast is a great example. He promotes BlueHost, a web hosting company, as he knows this product and knows his listeners will appreciate his recommendation.

- **Products or services** – Probably the best way to make money is by promoting your own products or services such as an e-book, short video tutorial, PDF guide, or coaching/consulting. Examples include Michael Hyatt's "Best Year Ever" course or John Lee Dumas "Podcaster's Paradise".

One successful podcaster who never thought they were going to be an entrepreneur is Adrienne Dorison. Her journey took her from blog to success strategist to podcaster. She hosts **The School of Self Mastery** podcast and also hosted a short series podcast called **The Pop-Up Podcast**.

Adrienne's Story

An initial interest in wildlife ecology and conservation saw Adrienne Dorison complete her undergraduate degree in this area. After completing her study, she ended up in a corporation doing supply chain work and project management. Adrienne's company trained her in Lean Six Sigma and consequently she became an expert in this area. Lean Six Sigma is a process that helps organisations be more efficient, remove waste from their process, and streamline operations.

Adrienne had goals of being a Vice President or CEO, although her path of personal growth led her to start a business on the side. She knew she had strong expertise to help people build an efficient, lean business and get greater results faster. Her first step was starting a blog, which began as more of a creative outlet and opportunity to talk about her passions such as change management, innovation, and leadership.

As the blog grew in popularity, Adrienne started forming relationships with her readers and offered free coaching sessions. This helped confirm she enjoyed coaching, but more importantly, she was able to help her clients achieve fantastic results. Her blog then turned organically into a business. Realising this was her passion, she set a goal to leave her corporate job to pursue her business full time.

For six months, Adrienne continued to build her business on the side. She was also focused on paying off her hefty $45,000 student loan before leaving her 9 to 5, highlighting a **sensible approach** to money management.

Adrienne is the first to tell you it was hard building a business on the side whilst working a corporate 9 to 5 job. She's also the first to admit her life was incredibly unbalanced during that period. Waking up a 4 a.m. to go to the gym, working in the morning before going to her corporate job, going to her corporate job and working there all day, sometimes squeezing in work in her lunch breaks. Once her corporate day was over, she was back working on her business in the evening, having client consultations in the evening and then working all weekend. It was an intense routine to say the least. But it was a short-term sacrifice she was willing to make because she had an end goal in sight.

Adrienne struggled to gain consistency with blogging. She was drawn to podcasting because she was a podcast listener herself. She started guest podcasting, that is, being interviewed by other entrepreneurs for their podcast. She realised how much she loved it, as well as how natural it felt. A key part of being an entrepreneur is creating content for your audience. For

Adrienne, podcasting was the perfect medium to enable her to create content, reach people, and build an audience.

Adrienne uses a combination of promoting her own products and services as well as affiliate marketing to profit from her podcast.

Why is podcasting so great?

❖ **It's a simple yet effective way to connect with people**

When you're building a business, *people buy from people they know, like, and trust.* The real, authentic you shines through on a podcast through your voice. People can hear the emotions, inflections, and emphasis as you speak. Getting your voice into people's heads is a great way to build a connection on a more intimate level.

❖ **It's an invaluable way to promote your business**

Podcasting is a great way to promote your business and build your email list and your influence. According to Pat Flynn of Smart Passive Income, "More and more people are discovering my brand through my podcast, and it continues to be the number one way that people discover me, more than SEO, Social Media, YouTube and links from other sites." Research has confirmed that 63% of listeners actually *purchased* something the podcast host had promoted.

❖ **It's growing in popularity**

According to the 2017 Infinite Dial Study by Edison Research and Triton Digital, 24% of Americans aged 12 or older say they have listened to a podcast in the past month, reflecting steady growth since 2013, when it was only 12%.

❖ **Podcasts are easily accessible by your audience**

All you need is a smartphone and you can download a podcast. The content is available at your fingertips and ready for you to digest.

The convenience of podcasts means you can listen to them *whenever* and *wherever you want*. Listeners can tune in on the train to work, while running, doing housework, or walking the dog.

❖ **You don't need to be an expert on your topic**

One of the great things about podcasting is that you don't actually need to be the guru on your topic. There are many ways to obtain information on your topic and it doesn't need to come from you. You can interview other experts and all you need to do is *ask insightful questions* from your listeners' point of view. You could even survey your audience to understand what topic they would like to know more on. Then find an expert in that topic and set up a time to interview them.

Adrienne's tips on how to actually get started

1. **What is your podcast about and who is your podcast for?**

   It's important to be clear and specific on your topic. Identify your target listener. Who are they? How will your podcast help them?

2. Decide on the format

There are many different ways to run your podcast. You could do interviews, top tips, how to's, or talk on a topic. Different formats include:

- **Solo** – this is where only you are talking. It's like a monologue and can be intimidating for you if you are just getting started.
- **Co-hosted** – this is presenting with a friend or business partner. It helps to have someone who you can bounce off and have robust discussions. Someone you have great rapport with will add to the listeners' experience.
- **Interviews** – this means talking to experts or people you admire. This can help to build your audience as people are drawn to your guest. Your guest will often have their own audience who might listen to the interview and subscribe to your show.

Listen to a number of different podcasts on a range of topics to get a feel for what others do and this will *help you* decide for yourself what format you want. Just like blogging, there are a ton of podcasts out there and you want to be able to stand out from others. Think about why someone should listen to your podcast versus someone else's.

3. Equipment

Keep things *simple* in the beginning. All you need is your computer with a built-in microphone and internet access. You can even use your iPhone or Android headphones. It's

146

better to get started and ensure you enjoy this before spending a large amount of money on equipment.

If you do wish to outlay some money on equipment, there's the Blue Mic microphone products such as the Yeti, which starts at US$130 or the Audio-Technica, which starts at US$80.

4. Recording / Editing

If you're going to be conducting interviews, then Skype is fine to use. However, you will need an add-on program to actually record the interview. Try Pamela (https://www.pamela.biz/shop/pamela_call_recorder_1) for PC users or eCamm Call Recorder (http://www.ecamm.com/mac/callrecorder/) for Mac users. Each has a one-off cost between $21.99 USD and $29.95 USD.

It's best to use free editing software to begin with, for example, you can download Audacity (http://www.audacityteam.org/) for both PC or Mac users. You can edit the podcast yourself or hire someone via Upwork or Fiverr to edit it for you.

5. Hosting

You will need a good media hosting service as podcasts are large audio files. There are a few options, with the most popular being:
- Libsyn (https://www.libsyn.com/)
- SoundCloud (https://soundcloud.com/)

- Blubrry
  (https://create.blubrry.com/resources/podcast-media-hosting/?code=wpbeginner)

Each will have various hosting plans with monthly fee. It's best to start small and upgrade as needed.

6. Submit your podcast to iTunes

Follow the step-by-step instructions from iTunes on how to submit your podcast to them:
https://itunespartner.apple.com/en/podcasts/overview

7. How often will you podcast?

As frequency can make a big impact on the overall success of your podcast, take some time to think carefully about this. Once a week is ideal. Consistency is really important as is the quality of the podcast.

8. How long should a podcast be?

No longer than one hour and no less than thirty minutes.

> The Cubicle Crusher's Hot Tip:
>
> Need a theme song for your podcast? Check out
> www.soundrangers.com or
> www.shockwave-sound.com

Adrienne's tips on how to achieve the heights of success with podcasting

1. Manage your energy

If you are still working a 9 to 5, then you might need to rethink how much you are actually giving to your job. This isn't about not performing or achieving in your role, it's about ensuring you still have *energy* to work on your side business without collapsing from burnout.

2. Coming up with content

If you don't have an established community, then think about your ideal audience and come up with questions they should be asking—then set about answering those. If you already have a free community of members on a forum such as Facebook, then look for the questions that they are asking.

The Cubicle Crusher's Hot Tip:

When it comes to your podcast, content is KING! Having great content that your audience wants will help your podcast be successful.

3. Create "show notes"

Podcast show notes offer a summary of the show content and direct people in order to increase traffic to your website. They also offer links to resources, products, or people. You can get the podcast transcribed or do it yourself in a blog post format.

4. Promote, promote, promote

Think about which social media platforms (such as Facebook, Twitter, or LinkedIn) your audience is on and use these to promote your podcast. If you've interviewed people, then reach out to them and ask whether they will share it with their audience.

5. Seek help

Podcasting has many components, some of which can be a bit technical. Try not to overcomplicate things. If you find yourself overwhelmed by it, then seek out help, either paid or using the internet to find resources to help move your podcast forward.

6. Enjoy podcasting

Whilst podcasting can be hard work, you *need* to have fun with it. Regularly check-in with yourself to ensure you enjoy it and you've still got a *passion* for it.

Where to find out more

You connect with Adrienne here:
- Website: www.adriennedorison.com
- Facebook: www.facebook.com/adriennedorisoncoach/
- Twitter: www.twitter.com/adriennedorison
- iTunes: https://itunes.apple.com/au/podcast/school-self-mastery-business/id1022041617?mt=2

Courses & articles:
- **"How to Download and Subscribe to Podcasts"** article by Sam Costello. Excellent step-by-step information on how to download, subscribe, and delete a podcast. Great for beginners! - https://www.lifewire.com/download-subscribe-to-podcasts-2000619
- **"The Podcast Workflow"** course by John Lee Dumas. This is a fantastic resource to help get you started with podcasting - https://www.eofire.com/the-podcast-workflow/
- **"5 of the best Podcasting Courses on the market"** article by Matthew McLean of The Podcast Host. This article lists some of the paid podcasting courses - https://www.thepodcasthost.com/training-development/best-podcasting-courses/

Chapter 11

Online Business Strategist

"Your work is going to fill a large part of your life, and the only way to be truly satisfied is to do what you believe is great work. And the only way to do great work is to love what you do. If you haven't found it yet, keep looking. Don't settle. As with all matters of the heart, you'll know when you find it. And, like any great relationship, it just gets better and better as the years roll on. So keep looking until you find it. Don't settle." – Steve Jobs

This chapter is for those who love business, love sharing their business knowledge with others, and want to help others create successful online businesses.

*

Where would we be without the internet? We can't imagine life without it, allowing us to do everything from paying bills to finding a place to live, booking holidays, researching for an assignment, and buying food and clothes. Not only has it enabled convenience for us as we live our lives, but it's also created a way for us to make money. The online business

152

world has opened up an array of possibilities for anyone wanting to start a business and put their knowledge and skills to good use.

This book is full of people who have all created online businesses in various niches and had amazing success. It's never been easier or cheaper to get your online business launched with done-for-you websites and hosting packages. Becoming an entrepreneur *is truly an option for everyone.*

One person who knew she was meant for the entrepreneurial world is Fabiola Giordani, a certified life and business coach, an author, speaker, and CEO of Fabiola Giordani International. She is an expert online business strategist, and was named by the *Huffington Post* as one of the 50 women entrepreneurs to follow in 2017 and *Empire Life* as one of the top virtual entrepreneurial influences and mentors.

Fabiola's Story

Fabiola was working her 9 to 5 when she began feeling like it was her time to do something different with her career and do something on her own. Her business journey started with eBay as she learnt about the online world. She then became a certified life and business coach, and set about starting her business in life coaching, although soon discovered this wasn't really for her. She realised she loved the coaching aspect, but felt she was negating her other talents of marketing and training. She continued to invest in herself through courses and learning about online marketing whilst still working her 9 to 5, which proved valuable when she came to launch her business.

In September 2014, Fabiola promptly quit her job. With no back-up plan, no money saved, and a cautious husband who was concerned about money, she gave herself 30 days to do nothing but work on her business. Starting with self-reflection, she asked herself, "How do I want to be remembered and what makes me happy?"

She quickly identified teaching and training, reflecting how anytime she got a job that after the initial training period, she would end up helping the trainer train other people. Making the connection with what excited her, she then considered the issues women were struggling with in their online business and developed some programs specific to this. With a basic website launched in her first 24 hours, she went on to make $10,000 in the next 21 days using her networking skills to source clients.

Fabiola credits her success in part to *hiring a coach*, as they propelled to get her out of the comfort zone. It also sped up her success, as she didn't have to spend a lot of time reading and taking a bunch of courses to get the knowledge she needed. She now runs a multiple six-figure (over half a million dollars) online business, which allows her to work from anywhere and support women in achieving their business dreams.

Why is being an online business strategist so great?

❖ You are utilising your strengths to help others build a successful online business.

❖ **Seeing the results and success of your clients.**

From amazing launches to media opportunities, your client's success will bring you a huge amount of motivation and pride.

❖ **Learning about other industries.**

Your clients will operate businesses across a number of industries and in many niches. As you help them make their businesses tick 24 hours a day, you will get exposure to other industries, keeping it interesting and varied.

❖ **Building a network of like-minded people.**

Creating a community of successful entrepreneurs who can leverage and lean-on each other whilst being guided by you is a very powerful movement.

Fabiola's tips on how to actually get started becoming an online business strategist

1. Know what you are good at

An online business strategist is a broad statement, so it's important to refine this down. A good way to do this is think what do you actually help people do? Is it getting more customers, creating a better marketing plan, or doing more implementation?

2. Be knowledgeable

You don't need to know everything; however, you do need to have an understanding of how a business works. If you have a gap in your knowledge, then take courses to help you *learn more* or know where you can connect with someone to help you get the knowledge.

Your clients are the experts in their industry and you don't need to be. For example, you might have a client who is a wedding planner, so you don't need to have experience as one. However, you might be great with defining a marketing strategy. So you bring your marketing expertise and knowledge to assist your client in their marketing strategy.

3. Master one area

Being too broad and focusing on all areas of business will overwhelm you and confuse your clients. *Niche down* to one or two areas such as branding and marketing. As you build your business and master other areas, you can add them in your offering, such as social media posting.

The Cubicle Crusher's Hot Tip:

FOCUS – Follow One Course Until Successful (Robert Kiyosaki)

Fabiola's tips on how to achieve the heights of success as an online business strategist

1. **Focus on the money-making activities**

   Implement the things that will give *you* the *results* you desire. For example, getting a new client versus trying to be on every social media platform. Get specific around the steps you need to take to generate actual income versus something that won't bring you any money.

2. **Connect with your audience**

   The money will come when you have great relationships in place and when you're focusing on providing your audience the *value*. Find some fun ways to connect with your audience and build a relationship with them such as webinars, live streaming, going to an actual event or a conference, or guest speaking.

3. **Find your point of difference**

   In the online world, it can be difficult to stand out from your competition. A key way to do this is to be different. Find that one thing that is unique to you or what you offer. For example, the first thing Fabiola does with her clients is to spend a whole day with them, where together, they create a strategy for the business.

> **The Cubicle Crusher's Hot Tip:**
>
> *Get creative in finding your point of difference. Look at the frustrations and needs of your clients. Also check out what your competitors aren't doing.*

4. Have the right systems in place

Establish systems for your business so if you take a vacation or get sick and you hire someone, they can easily and quickly understand how you work. This may be knowing the payment structure, how to set up a webinar, or how to set up an interview. Creating systems makes it much easier for you to run your business or for someone to step in and run it on your behalf.

5. Be confident

If you want to stand out, you need to *be confident* in what you do so when you are ready to ask for the sale, they feel that confidence and will buy from you. If you're confident in the results that you can give others, then your potential clients will believe they can get the results.

Where to find out more

You can connect with Fabiola here:

- Website: www.fabiolagiordani.com

- Facebook: www.facebook.com/fabiolagiordani/
- Instagram: www.instagram.com/fabiolaygiordani

Chapter 12

The Magic of a Membership Site

"Epic things start with small humble steps. Pay respect to your beginnings. And if you're just starting out, know that it's okay to be sucky. To be small. To be messy and chaotic. Just make sure to never ever stop dreaming." – Vishen Lakhiani

---

This chapter is for people who are after recurring income, are consistent in creating content, and want to impact a lot of people at a time.

*

According to Yaro Starak of www.entrepeneurs-journey.com, "Membership sites are the best online business model". Lindsay Flanagan of www.memberpress.com also echoes this point saying, "A membership site is one of the best ways to form an online business."

So what is a membership site? According to Lindsay Flanagan (www.memberpress.com), "A membership site is a gated part of your online business where only members who subscribe can access the content you've placed behind the gates. A "gate" is simply a barrier you build into your website using a plugin."

Membership sites are ***an amazing way*** to earn income. Not just a source of income, but a **recurring** source of income. In the world of business, it certainly helps to have a regular source of income on a monthly basis. One person who knows all about the world of membership sites is Dwayne Kerr. Dwayne is a life and entrepreneur coach who had amazing success through interviewing 24 experts on the law of attraction. He placed these interviews (MP3 recordings) on a membership site, which generated $15,000 GBP a month in recurring income.

Dwayne's Story

Dwayne felt from a very young age that he desired the freedom to do what and when he wanted. This included travelling the world and experiencing the good things in life. Not to mention being able to sleep in on a Monday instead of having to rush to work.

Dwayne's entrepreneurial journey started whilst growing up in London. After school, he began building his online career doing internet marketing and was starting to earn money online. He had started creating his own products when he came upon an ad for an internet marketing seminar run by Mark Anastasi. He attended the event and even managed to chat with Mark and share what he was building via the internet. Mark commended him for taking action and his success.

Whilst he was earning some money off eBay, he realised he could add more value to his online business by applying the learning from the seminar. Having drawn so much inspiration from both Mark and the seminar, he realised he needed to be around more like-minded people to expand upon his success to date.

Keen to take his business to the next level, Dwayne had already developed a strong interest in the personal development field. He had been interviewing experts and then offering the interviews to his audience for free. This helped him to build a following and an email list. He realised if he took the interviews, started packaging them in a different way, attached a dollar value to them, and developed a marketing plan, he would be able to earn income off the interviews.

Following Mark's advice, he gave out one of the interviews for free to attract people to his site. He then put the other recordings on a membership site, which could be accessed for $27 a month. Every month, he does a new interview. He has now managed to build his site to 500 members, earning him $15,000 a month in recurring income.

Why are membership sites so great?

❖ **Recurring income**

One of the best things about a membership site is recurring income. You charge a monthly or yearly fee to members for access to your content. For example, say you charge $47 per month and you have 100 members, that's $4,700 per month of income. Increase your members to 500 per month and you earn $23,500 per month. It's easy to see how a membership site provides a liveable monthly income.

❖ You build a community

Through sharing your experiences, both good and not so good, *you* are being relatable to your members and creating a unique, useful community. You can ask your members to share their own experiences and responses, which helps to build a group of like-minded people. This interaction can be *very powerful* in creating a community who support and learn from each other as well as from you.

❖ Increases the value of your content

It's human nature to place a higher perceived value over something we need to pay a premium for versus something that is low in cost, or free. Limiting access to some of your content via a membership site *increases* the value of your top-notch expertise. Of course, you can't simply offer any content. It is important that what you are offering is high quality and of value to your members.

❖ They're not hard to set up

Setting up a website has never been easier, especially with all the technology today. The popular WordPress platform can host your membership site. WordPress has plugins for membership control, chat rooms, video support, and forums to assist you in creating your membership site.

The Cubicle Crusher's Hot Tip:

Did you know what a content gateway is?
It's essentially a barrier between the visitors
to your site and some of your content. A
membership site is an example of this.

Dwayne's tips on how to actually get started with a membership site

1. Choose a topic or niche

Find your undeniable passion for something that you want to share with others. *Passion is essential to ensure you have the energy to keep going.* You need to be in it for the long haul.

Check to see whether there is a magazine, or a Google, Yahoo, Facebook, or LinkedIn group talking about your topic or niche. You are basically researching to ensure there is demand.

The key is to ensure what you're offering is specialised enough that people will pay for your content and services. It's also important to find what's unique and different to your site compared to other sites on the same or a similar topic.

2. What content will you deliver? How often?

High quality content is *essential* for your members. Common forms of content are audio, text, and video. Text could include blog posts, special reports, or PDFs. Audio could be expert interviews, podcasts, webinars, coaching calls, or audio lessons. Video could also be webinars, virtual conferences, or training videos.

What also makes content valuable is the efficiency of the results you create. For example, 7-minute abs, healthy meals in 20 minutes or less, or how to make an extra $1,000 a month. What content you deliver and the type of content will depend on your topic or niche.

Next, you will need to decide on a content delivery schedule. It can be tempting to want to share your content faster than your members can devour it. If your members can't keep up with the content, they'll get frustrated and cancel their membership.

3. Build your membership base

An important step for any membership site owner is finding people who are willing to pay a fee every month. It would be nice to sit back and wait for the traffic to start arriving at your membership site, however you need to be proactive. Collect names and email addresses to build your list and communicate with them each time you have something new to share or an update.

One strategy is to allow people to sign up for free. Let a handful of people in for free or offer a week's free trial.

It's worth taking some time to develop a *membership marketing strategy* and this could include holding free online events, guest posting on other blogs in your niche, setting up an affiliate program, and paid advertising. You can also invest in some training to assist you in your efforts.

4.   Set up the software

You will need to have a website established such as on WordPress. Chapter 7 on blogging provides links to establish a website.

There are many different software options or plugins available for membership sites. The goal is to keep it simple. Do your research to understand the options available. You want to ensure the software or plugin you obtain can do the following:

- Set up pricing, login, account, and thank you pages for your users.
- Add membership plans at any time.
- Content access control. That is, restrict access to content including posts, pages, categories, tags, and files.
- Content dripping, which allows you to show restricted content to members after a certain time.
- Integration with email services such as AWeber or MailChimp and podcast hosting.
- Take payment via a payment gateway such as PayPal or Stripe.

5. Interact and engage with members

Part of the reason members join a site is because they know they get access to the owner, which is *you*. This helps develop a stronger reason to join and stay part of your site. This could mean:

- A private Facebook group where you connect and chat with members
- Posting regularly on social media to assist and support your members
- A Facebook Live post sharing something or answering a question
- A live webinar where your members can ask questions

Dwayne's tips on how to achieve the heights of success with membership sites

1. Don't be perfect

When developing content for your membership site, it's easy to caught up in a "perfectionist" way of thinking. Simply put, you want to ensure that what you are sharing with your members is of a high standard and of great value to them. Be conscious of how high a standard you are holding yourself to. This isn't about releasing crap content, but choose **progress over perfection**. It doesn't need to be absolutely perfect, but 80% or 85% is good enough. Get your content out and start giving your members value.

2. Think outside the content box

When it comes to great content, there are many ways to develop this and show your members great value. Here are some ideas for content:

- **Reviews** - Complete a book review
- **Profiles** – you could profile a member or another expert
- **Solve a problem** – help one of your members with a problem
- **News** – recap any major stories in your chosen topic area or niche
- **Accountability partners** – encourage your members to find an accountability partner to hold themselves accountable for completing their goals
- **Link posts** – list of links to other resources
- **Creative or fun projects** – get creative with something your members can participate in or complete, for example, a mini-challenge for a week
- **Case studies** – of different situations or success stories
- Inspirational or motivational stories
- **Survey your members** – ask them what information they want

3. Pricing

How do you decide what to charge? How do you put a value on your content? This is one of the trickiest steps and it's advisable to invest time to get it right.

169

Take a look at other membership sites to understand what others are charging. This is the best form of market research you can do before you launch. Reach out and connect with them to ask what they priced their site at.

There are a broad range of pricing points from $3.95 up to $5,000 per month. The best way to determine the right price is to put something out there and charge for it. People *need* to feel they are getting value and you want your offer to be perceived as *high value*. You can make the mistake of pricing your site too low. There could be a number of reasons for this, such as fear of failure or low self-esteem. But pricing too low can be detrimental to your site.

4.   The "best way forward"

Here's hoping your journey to building your membership site is all plain sailing. But chances are, there'll be a hiccup along the way or something you've not encountered before. It might be a technical issue or personal issue that impacts on the time you have. Regardless of what comes up for you, all you need to do is step back and think, what's the best way forward? Who could help me with my issue?

5.   Be adaptable and seek feedback

Always remember, a membership site is for your members. So, it's important to seek their feedback—both constructive and supportive. Listen to what they have to say. It's no good pursuing something if your members don't care for it. Run a regular members survey or ask a few targeted questions in your Facebook group, for example, which do you find more valuable: profiles or case studies? What would you like to see more of?

Set aside time, for example every six months, to regularly review your site. Your site will evolve and grow, so investing time to assess what's working and what's not is essential to your long-term success.

> The Cubicle Crusher's Hot Tip:
>
> Why not make a welcome video for your members? Walk them through the site and remind them of all the benefits to joining. Plus, it adds a personal touch.

6. Member retention

One of the challenges with membership sites is that people can opt-out or unsubscribe, so you need to consider how you will maintain your numbers. A lot of this comes down to *promoting your site*.

Another strategy is the concept of a strategic product staircase. That is, having different levels of membership available, for example, gold, diamond, or platinum levels. Each level is priced differently and offers additional inclusions. So your top membership level is the most expensive, but also offers the most value. This allows your members to choose which level is of interest to them and which level they can comfortably afford.

If you had someone in your top-level program want to leave or opt out, you could offer them to move into a different level, which may be more affordable for them. This helps you to retain the member and some income, and keep them happy.

If you get a lot of members opting-out, then connect with them and ask why they want to leave, and what you can do to keep them? Seeking your members feedback is crucial to ensure you are consistently offering great value.

Where to find out more

You can connect with Dwayne here:
- Website: www.ibusinessmastermind.com
- Twitter: https://twitter.com/DwayneKerr
- LinkedIn: https://uk.linkedin.com/in/dwaynekerr

Courses and websites:
- **"How to Launch a Membership Site"** a six-part blog post by Yaro Starak of www.entrepreneurs-journey.com - This is a fantastic resource!
  - Part 1 – Build Your Pre-eminence - https://www.entrepreneurs-journey.com/704/how-to-launch-a-membership-site-part-1-build-your-preeminence/
  - Part 2 – Communication Channels - https://www.entrepreneurs-journey.com/707/how-to-launch-a-membership-site-part-2-communication-channels/

- o   Part 3 – Technology - https://www.entrepreneurs-journey.com/710/how-to-launch-a-membership-site-part-3-technology/
- o   Part 4 – Content and Pricing - https://www.entrepreneurs-journey.com/713/how-to-launch-a-membership-site-part-4-content-and-pricing/
- o   Part 5 – Triggers - https://www.entrepreneurs-journey.com/719/how-to-launch-a-membership-site-part-5-triggers/

- **"Launch a membership site in 90 days"** course by Jonathan Milligan of Blogging Your Passion. At the time of printing, this course is priced at $200USD - https://members.bloggingyourpassion.com/store/q7jzojee

- **Members Site Academy** - http://www.membersiteacademy.com/

- **The Membership Guys** - https://www.themembershipguys.com

"When you grow up you tend to get told the world is the way it is and to live your life inside the world. Try not to bash into the walls too much. Try to have a nice family, have fun, save a little money. That's a very limited life. Life can be much broader once you discover one simple fact. Everything around you that you call life was made up by people that were no smarter than you and you can change it, you can influence it, you can build your own things that other people can use. Once you learn that, you'll never be the same again." – Steve Jobs

Acknowledgements

I wish to thank my parents Warwick and Barbara for all their support and encouragement. I wouldn't be who I am without your love and guidance.

To my mentor, Mark Anastasi, thank you for the amazing opportunity. Here's to emulating your success!

To my editor, Ameesha Green, thank you for your feedback, wisdom, and ability to assist me to ensure my writing is succinct so others understand what I am saying.

To my friends, who have put up with hearing about this for about a year. It's finally done!!

References

Introduction:

- http://www.mckinsey.com/business-functions/digital-mckinsey/our-insights/four-fundamentals-of-workplace-automation
- http://www.forbes.com/sites/elainepofeldt/2015/05/25/shocker-40-of-workers-now-have-contingent-jobs-says-u-s-government/#6271a0162532
- https://www.theguardian.com/sustainable-business/2016/sep/26/humans-are-going-to-have-the-edge-over-robots-where-work-demands-creativity
- http://www.inc.com/peter-economy/19-interesting-hiring-statistics-you-should-know.html
- http://www.forbes.com/sites/dailymuse/2015/12/07/6-insider-job-search-facts-thatll-make-you-re-think-how-youre-applying/2/#3d2dd8fe146e
- http://www.roymorgan.com/findings/6968-roy-morgan-unemployment-august-2016-201609141843
- http://www.gallup.com/businessjournal/188033/worldwide-employee-engagement-crisis.aspx)
- http://www.telegraph.co.uk/finance/jobs/11871751/Its-official-most-people-are-miserable-at-work.html
- https://www.linkedin.com/pulse/80-people-linkedin-dont-enjoy-hate-job-dan-thomas).

Mindset:
- https://www.entrepreneur.com/article/236465

Starting Your Business:

- http://www.huffingtonpost.com.au/entry/5-really-good-reasons-to-take-a-personality-test_us_55d21e55e4b055a6dab0f34a
- https://www.16personalities.com/free-personality-test

Social Media:

- http://www.socialmediatoday.com/content/what-social-media-manager
- http://www.smartinsights.com/social-media-marketing/social-media-strategy/new-global-social-media-research/
- https://problogger.com/what-is-affiliate-marketing/
- http://neilpatel.com/blog/beginners-guide-how-to-build-a-killer-instagram-following-and-increase-your-sales/
- http://socialmarketingwriting.com/complete-guide-successful-social-media-manager/
- https://www.womensnetwork.com.au/corinna_essa_upfront
- http://www.business2community.com/social-media/47-superb-social-media-marketing-stats-facts-01431126#ayvcr1zemzrt9ugz.99
- https://www.brandwatch.com/blog/96-amazing-social-media-statistics-and-facts-for-2016/
- http://www.clickbank.com/
- https://sproutsocial.com/insights/social-media-tips/

Affiliate Marketing with Twitter:

- https://www.statista.com/statistics/282087/number-of-monthly-active-twitter-users/
- https://www.omnicoreagency.com/twitter-statistics/
- https://support.twitter.com/articles/13920
- https://webtegrity.com/our-blog/social-media-marketing/whats-difference-between-facebook-and-twitter/
- https://smartasset.com/career/how-to-make-money-on-twitter
- http://charlesmoney.com/posting-affiliate-links-on-twitter/
- https://monetizepros.com/features/101-ways-to-make-money-with-twitter/#success
- https://www.dailydot.com/business/5-tips-making-money-twitter/
- https://idonsabi.com/2017/01/05/how-to-make-money-online-with-twitter/
- http://siragsoft.com/learn-how-to-create-marketing-success-with-twitter/
- https://alloutlivin.com/2016/12/19/how-to-live-your-dream-life-affiliate-marketing-success-stories/
- http://marketingstrategyx.com/affiliate-marketing-with-social-media/
- https://problogger.com/8-tips-for-affiliate-marketers-on-using-twitter/
- http://www.monetise.co.uk/affiliate-marketers-guide-making-money-twitter-ads/
- https://www.authorityhacker.com/best-affiliate-programs/

- http://www.accelerationpartners.com/blog/affiliate-marketing-101-part-i
- https://aworkathomejobs.com/twitter-is-very-powerful-learn-how-to-market-your-affiliate-link
- http://101geek.com/how-to-make-money-with-twitter/
- https://techforluddites.com/hashtag/

Writing Books:

- https://thewritelife.com/self-publishing-on-amazon-450000/
- https://www.ircomediary.com/7-things-learned-publishing-book
- http://www.huffingtonpost.com/juliana-maio/five-reasons-why-everybody-should-write-a-book_b_6278520.html
- https://www.amarketingexpert.com/writing-book-can-transform-business/
- https://melissaambrosini.com/wealth/4-reasons-why-writing-a-book-will-boost-your-business/
- http://strategicfactory.com/about-us/blog/news_archive.html/article/2017/01/09/6-reasons-your-business-should-write-a-book
- http://authority.pub/steps-to-writing-a-book/
- https://www.dangerandplay.com/2015/07/24/how-to-sell-10000-copies-of-a-book/
- http://www.thecreativepenn.com/2012/10/12/help-my-book-isnt-selling/
- https://www.forbes.com/sites/nickmorgan/2013/11/05/how-to-market-and-sell-your-book-in-five-steps/2/#c693C506ebaa

- http://www.huffingtonpost.com/penny-c-sansevieri/how-to-sell-morebooks-without-spending-a-dime_b_8273446.html
- http://www.mackcollier.com/so-how-much-money-will-you-make-from-writing-a-book/
- https://goinswriter.com/tips-writing-book/
- https://pressbooks.com/blog/how-to-line-up-reviews-for-your-book-launch/

Ebooks:

- https://www.statista.com/topics/1474/e-books/
- http://www.masculinedevelopment.com/how-to-sell-ebooks-online-for-passive-income/
- http://onlineincometeacher.com/money/how-to-make-money-by-writing-an-ebook/
- https://www.thebalance.com/how-to-write-and-publish-an-ebook-1360713
- http://www.moneycrashers.com/write-publish-ebook/
- http://workfromhomehappiness.com/write-an-ebook-in-5-steps-and-start-earning-passive-income/
- https://www.freedomwithwriting.com/freedom/uncategorized/8-reasons-every-writer-should-write-an-ebook/
- https://justagirlandherblog.com/why-you-should-write-and-launch-an-ebook/
- http://pajamaproductivity.com/write-awesome-ebooks/
- http://diseasecalleddebt.com/how-to-create-an-ebook/
- http://writetodone.com/how-market-ebooks/

- http://authorearnings.com/report/february-2017/
- http://www.telegraph.co.uk/lifestyle/11789876/meet-the-kindlepreneurs.html
- https://www.theguardian.com/books/2012/jan/12/amanda-hocking-self-publishing
- http://www.selfpublishingquestions.com/word-count/
- https://www.thebalance.com/make-money-selling-ebooks-online-4122181

Online Courses:

- http://blog.teachable.com/make-money-online#pointer17
- https://www.businessinsider.com.au/rob-percival-online-coding-courses-2015-2?r=us&ir=t
- https://www.entrepreneur.com/article/239622
- http://sociallysorted.com.au/how-to-create-an-online-course/
- http://blog.thinkific.com/10-steps-creating-successful-online-course/
- https://www.forbes.com/sites/dorieclark/2014/08/06/how-to-create-a-money-making-online-course/#2d17e9917c23
- https://www.videoschoolonline.com/9-reasons-teaching-online-courses-is-the-best-way-to-make-passive-income/
- http://oneyeartofreedom.com/online-income/
- https://www.learnworlds.com/how-much-money-can-you-make-selling-online-courses/

Coaching:

- http://www.forbes.com/sites/ashleystahl/2016/04/25/busting-the-top-5-myths-about-the-coaching-industry/#3f1c0a721f1c
- https://mesiti.com/building-a-7-figure-coaching-business/
- http://www.48days.com/7-reasons-i-love-being-a-coach/
- http://www.coachville.com/connect/top-10-reasons-to-coach/
- http://www.coachuaustralasia.com/become-a-coach/benefits/
- http://coachestrainingblog.com/becomeacoach/more-than-10-reason-1-10-to-become-a-coach/
- http://www.metasysteme-coaching.eu/english/why-do-you-want-to-become-a-coach-and-how-to-do-it/
- http://liveboldandbloom.com/05/life-coaching/how-to-become-life-coach
- https://jessicanazarali.com/how-i-made-355k-in-6-months-as-a-coach-and-how-you-can-too/
- https://russruffino.com/marketing/10-rules-for-making-200000k-per-month-as-a-coach-or-consultant/
- http://www.success.com/mobile/article/inside-the-coaching-industry
- http://www.huffingtonpost.com/entry/3-lessons-from-surviving-a-heart-attack-at-28_us_579b2425e4b00e7e269f08ae
- http://www.trainingzone.co.uk/deliver/coaching/nine-things-you-must-do-before-starting-your-own-coaching-business
- https://coachfederation.org/blog/index.php/8091/
- http://southerncrosscoaching.com.au/10-practical-tips-to-build-a-successful-coaching-business/

- http://www.kelliederuyter.com/step-by-step_new_coach_action_guide.pdf
- http://www.noomii.com/coach-blog/life-coach-salary-100000
- https://jennscalia.com/six-figure-coaches/
- https://erickson.edu/blog/icf-coaching-industry-infographic-profile-2016
- https://fizzle.co/sparkline/how-to-coaching-business

Blogging:

- https://hostingfacts.com/internet-facts-stats-2016/
- https://wordpress.com/activity/
- https://startbloggingonline.com/
- https://problogger.com/7-blogging-mistakes-to-avoid-in-2017/
- https://www.bloggingbasics101.com/how-do-i-start-a-blog/
- https://solvid.co.uk/blogging-in-2017/
- http://rebelgrowth.com/top-earning-blogs/
- https://bloggerspassion.com/bloggers-income-report-how-much-money-do-top-bloggers-make-and-how/
- https://coschedule.com/blog/how-to-be-a-successful-blogger/
- https://allbloggingtips.com/want-to-become-a-famous-blogger-then-read-this/
- http://www.trafficgenerationcafe.com/popular-blogs-from-scratch/

eCommerce – Part 1 - eBay:

- http://mashable.com/2010/08/07/ebay-facts/#odXHhxOpgkqB

- https://www.statista.com/topics/2181/ebay/
- https://www.salehoo.com/blog/ebay-success-story
- http://www.dailymail.co.uk/femail/article-3221228/how-fortune-home-woman-makes-25-million-year-ebay-reveals-tips-earning-cash-online-says-people-3-000-worth-items-just-lying-around.html
- https://www.forbes.com/sites/marciaturner/2017/02/08/how-one-ebay-millionaire-makes-a-living-selling-designer-clothing-shoes-and-accessories/#37f742b22287
- https://theworkathomewife.com/7-tips-making-living-ebay/
- http://www.quickanddirtytips.com/business-career/small-business/can-you-really-make-money-on-ebay
- http://escapologist.com.au/category/make-money-online/make-money-on-ebay/
- https://www.mybusiness.com.au/technology/213-eight-ways-to-succeed-on-ebay-australia
- http://howsbusiness.org/business-articles/running-an-ebay-business
- https://crazylister.com/content/ebay-doctor-how-to-sell-on-ebay/
- https://hubpages.com/business/how-to-make-money-online-by-selling-on-ebay-steps-to-list-and-sell-your-items-from-around-the-house
- http://www.savethestudent.org/make-money/ebay-selling-tips.html
- https://ilovetobeselling.com/top-secret-to-sales-success-on-ebay/

eCommerce – Part 2 – Online Stores & Amazon :

- http://fortune.com/2016/06/08/online-shopping-increases/
- https://www.entrepreneur.com/article/251386
- https://www.shopify.com.au/blog/14459769-ecommerce-business-blueprint-how-to-build-launch-and-grow-a-profitable-online-store
- http://neilpatel.com/blog/from-start-to-profit-how-to-setup-an-ecommerce-store-and-generating-sales/
- http://shopifynation.com/entrepreneurship/how-to-start-a-successful-ecommerce-store/
- http://www.contentlaunch.com/sites/default/files/E Book%20-%20Guide%20to%20Building%20an%20Ecommerce%20Business.pdf
- http://mywifequitherjob.com/the-best-way-to-find-vendors-for-your-online-store/
- http://memarketingservices.com/how-to-start-an-ecommerce-business-6-easy-tips/
- https://founderu.selz.com/12-tips-starting-ecommerce-business/
- https://www.entrepreneur.com/article/246223
- https://www.entrepreneur.com/article/248142
- https://www.referralcandy.com/blog/6-habits-ecommerce-owners/
- https://7pillarsofsellingonline.com/how-to-sell-on-amazon-the-best-kept-secret/
- http://thesellingfamily.com/beginners-guide-starting-amazon-fba-business/

- https://www.vpnmentor.com/blog/vital-internet-trends/
- http://www.krishaweb.com/blog/9-reasons-you-should-start-an-e-commerce-business
- http://www.top10ecommercesitebuilders.com/?utm_source=google&kw=ecommerce%20platform&c=168824688618&t=search&p=&m=b&adpos=1t2&dev=c&devmod=&mobval=0&network=g&campaignid=203962143&adgroupid=14900841063&targetid=aud-287900310926:kwd-47715960&interest=&physical=9056931&feedid=&a=529&ts=&gclid=CPGt85vX2tMCFRObvQodlUoJwQ

Podcasting:

- https://goleansixsigma.com/what-is-lean-six-sigma/
- https://blog.spinweb.net/facts-about-business-podcasting-that-will-blow-your-mind
- http://www.edisonresearch.com/iab-edison-research-podcast-advertising-study-2016/
- http://www.journalism.org/2016/06/15/podcasting-fact-sheet/
- http://www.copyblogger.com/why-start-podcast/
- http://www.dictionary.com/browse/podcast
- https://www.postplanner.com/6-revealing-reasons-why-podcasting-no-brainer-for-business/
- https://www.entrepreneurs-journey.com/230/what-is-a-podcast/
- https://www.entrepreneur.com/article/290441
- https://blog.patreon.com/make-money-podcasting/
- http://www.convinceandconvert.com/social-media-measurement/the-5-key-2016-podcast-statistics/

- http://adage.com/article/digitalnext/podcast-predictions/307210/
- http://podcastfast.com/how-to-make-money-podcasting/
- https://theaudacitytopodcast.com/how-podcasters-are-making-money-with-podcasting-tap206/
- http://cranberry.fm/blog/how-often-should-you-podcast
- https://www.eofire.com/the-podcast-workflow/
- http://www.wpbeginner.com/wp-tutorials/step-by-step-guide-how-to-start-a-podcast-with-wordpress/
- http://yourpodcastguru.com/how-to-create-content-for-your-podcast/
- https://www.thepodcasthost.com/websites-hosting/what-format-should-podcast-shownotes-be-written-in-podcasting-qa/
- http://blog.hubstaff.com/start-a-podcast/

Membership Sites:

- https://www.entrepreneurs-journey.com/1062/the-truth-about-membership-sites/
- https://www.memberpress.com/membership-sites-101/
- https://monetizepros.com/membership-sites/guide-to-subscription-revenue/
- https://ambitionally.com/increase-online-sales/creating-membership-sites/membership-site-examples/
- https://ambitionally.com/increase-online-sales/creating-membership-sites/membership-site-benefits/

- http://www.matthewwoodward.co.uk/tutorials/start-profitable-membership-site-step-step/
- https://www.memberpress.com/5-reasons-every-blogger-should-start-a-membership-site/
- http://www.mumpreneursonline.com/how-to/10-reasons-to-start-a-membership-site
- https://www.locationrebel.com/membership-site-questions/
- https://www.memberpress.com/membership-sites-101/
- http://bloggingyourpassion.com/how-to-start-a-membership-site-in-8-simple-steps/
- http://www.matthewwoodward.co.uk/tutorials/start-profitable-membership-site-step-step/
- https://www.memberpress.com/how-to-build-a-customer-base-for-your-premium-membership-site/
- http://www.copyblogger.com/membership-site-basics/
- http://membershipexpert.com/creating-great-content/20-types-of-content-you-can-write-about-in-your-membership-site-372/#more-372
- https://problogger.com/how-to-create-a-membership-program-that-rocks/
- https://www.themembershipguys.com/figure-charge-membership-site/
- https://www.entrepreneurs-journey.com/713/how-to-launch-a-membership-site-part-4-content-and-pricing/
- https://premium.wpmudev.org/blog/membership-site-tools/?utm_expid=3606929-108.o6f5ypxutg-xpcv9sy1yrw.0&utm_referrer=https%3a%2f%2fwww.google.com.au%2f

www.ingramcontent.com/pod-product-compliance
Lightning Source LLC
Chambersburg PA
CBHW071551200326
41519CB00021BB/6693